RATCATCHER

Ratcatcher

LYNNE RAMSAY

faber and faber
LONDON·NEW YORK

First published in 1999
by Faber and Faber Limited
Bloomsbury House, 74-77 Great Russell Street, London WC1B 3DA

Published in the United States by Faber and Faber Inc.
a division of Farrar, Straus and Giroux Inc., New York

Photoset by Parker Typesetting Service, Leicester
Printed and bound by CPI Group (UK) Ltd, Croydon, CR0 4YY

A CIP record for this book is available
from the British Library

ISBN 978-0-571-20349-9

The publisher would like to thank
Gavin Emerson and Tom Vincent-Townend
for their help with this book.

CONTENTS

FOREWORD

Anyone who has seen *Ratcatcher* (the film) will see that in many ways the script is different in terms of structure, omitted scenes, etc. I have decided to leave the script as it was in the final stages before shooting, as I feel that this is more informative than a scripted version of the film in its finished form. It always bugs me when I read a straight rendition of a film, as I can hardly believe that no changes were made as a result of the film-making process. In the hope, then, that this will prove a more useful document and companion piece to the film, I leave the script – warts and all. Proofreading the text, I have found it difficult to stop myself rewriting the whole thing. This is very easy in hindsight.

During filming, scenes were dropped for a variety of reasons: Rained off. Rained off. Rained off. I was having a bad day. Someone else was having a bad day. Everybody was having a bad day. No time. No money. Rained off again. Or they just plain didn't work . . .

Anything additional in the film materialized on the day. Some were happy accidents, some improvisations, and a few rare brainwaves in desperate moments. I cannot take all the credit for the best of these; they were often suggestions from the cast and crew I was lucky enough to work with.

Structure-wise, the editor Lucia Zucchetti and I tried to find some coherence in the jumble of material amassed when we cut on a Steinbeck (in an Avid amount of time). Cutting on film is slower but we prefer it, and we would happily have spent another month or two getting it just right. Who said that a film is never finished, just abandoned? I still dream of the perfect version that disappeared somewhere between my head and the big screen. Maybe next time.

Lynne Ramsay
October 1999

CHILDHOOD IS A BLANK CANVAS
An Interview with Lynne Ramsay by Lizzie Francke

Lynne Ramsay was born in Glasgow in 1969. She graduated in photography from Napier University in Edinburgh and then attended the National Film and Television School. There she studied cinematography, before switching to the directing course. In 1995 her graduation short film, *Small Deaths*, was selected for competition at Cannes, where it won the Prix du Jury. Her second short, *Kill the Day* (1996), confirmed that Ramsay was a director with an extraordinary, original talent. She returned to Cannes in 1997 with a third short, *Gasman*, which also won the Prix du Jury.

In her early work Ramsay explored the family and the nature of growing up, combining documentary-like observation with an eye for details both abstract and absurd. Ramsay understands emotional mood and moment, and in each frame draws the viewer's eye to some gesture that can be at once casual and momentous. With her debut feature *Ratcatcher* Ramsay continues her artistic project to create a cinema that brings together both the social and the surreal to profound effect.

LIZZIE FRANCKE: *It seems to be me that* Ratcatcher *grows out of your previous short films* Kill the Day *and* Small Deaths, *in that both shorts examine the fragility of evolving as a human being. They're both about observing characters move from childhood through adolescence to adulthood, and as they do so their world becomes darker.*
LYNNE RAMSAY: I think there are elements of the feature that have grown out of the short films I've made. It wasn't particularly intentional, but I can see it more clearly now. *Ratcatcher* has similar concerns – in terms of subject matter and I guess in terms of style, theme and characterizations, as well as my continued work with non-professional actors. You can definitely see the seed as in the earlier work. I knew for my first feature that I had to draw on what I had learned already and what I knew worked for me. To try to reinvent yourself as a film-maker at this stage is a big mistake – though ironically that is what people ask of you if they

find your working method does not fit into the conventional system of feature film production.

Why do you think that you have been so preoccupied with childhood?
For me childhood is an interesting time because your opinions are not yet set. Perhaps you see the world around you more clearly and openly, in a simpler way, without the baggage of moral judgement. It is interesting to see the absurdity of the adult world from this point of view. Childhood is like a blank canvas, in terms of the direction you can take for good or bad. I enjoy working with non-professional child actors for similar reasons. They are open to the process, without baggage, and so anything can happen. I think the best actors also psych into this state of being. Some photographers have a similar fascination with the world, as if they are seeing everything as if for the first time. I don't want to be pigeonholed as a film-maker who makes films about childhood. My next projects are moving in different directions but personally, and as a director, I try to look at things from a child's point of view.

Why did you set the film during the dustmen's strike of the 1970s?
I was fascinated by the setting – it was the starting point of the film. It was something I vaguely remembered when I was growing up. I was not using the strike in order to make a social comment. It has been put to me that the politics of the strike are not dealt with in the film, but a boy like James would hardly be concerned with politics, would he? I looked at some photographs from that time and they were quite surreal – kids pulling things from the rubbish, dressing up, finding old dolls, killing rats. It sounds grotesque, but relating back to the previous question, it all depends on your point of view. People were really poor (the pictures sometimes look mediaeval) and people still are. But growing up in a place like that can also be magical. You make the best you can of your environment. I don't think it kills your imagination.

What I find interesting is that the viewer isn't very conscious of the period setting. It's not a retro film.
I wanted to make the film seem timeless, which is something I discussed in depth with the designer Jane Morton and the cinematographer Alwin Kuchler. We didn't want all the kitsch

nostalgia of the 1970s (which seems to appear in quite a lot of films set in this period) to get in the way of creating a believable setting. In the kind of environment we were describing, people would not be wearing bang-up-to-date clothing or have bang-up-to-date furniture. We mixed elements of the fifties, sixties and seventies; ironically it looks more authentically seventies because we took this stance. I always tried to look for an unusual point of view, not always what you would expect to see. Even when the point of view is objective, we thought it should have something strange and childlike about it – to try to find some kind of beauty in what appears, at first sight, ugly.

The world you create in this film is like an island. We know it's Glasgow because we've been told it is, and one recognizes the tenements, but it could be anywhere. There's a very real sense of place but there's symbolism too, with the rubbish and the ominously murky canal juxtaposed with the Elysium-like new housing estate on the edge of the city. And you use a palette of colours to back this up.
It was important to me that the film wasn't too parochial, because this place exists all over but in different forms. I very consciously avoided straight social realism and when people categorize the film as such, I feel that's a real misinterpretation.

The film is very much about space, and the lack of space in a family home and the surrounding environment.
In the scene where James takes the bus to the new housing estate, I wanted it to seem like the first time he has ever seen a field and so much open space. Coming from an overcrowded environment it would feel like heaven on earth.

The moment when Kenny's mouse Snowball flies off to the moon works brilliantly. There is a psychological realism to the fantasy.
I wasn't sure I should include this in the film, even though I'd written the scene. It sat pretty oddly. It is the one moment where we break into total dreamscape. I decided to use the shot because it allows even the most cruel situation to lead into a childish fantasy – still maintaining an innocence, a breathing space in a relentless environment.

How did you develop the central character of James?
I wanted to make the main character a boy. There is more peer

pressure on boys to collude in a pack mentality and become desensitized in this sort of tough environment. There is very little opportunity for emotional release. James does not want to end up like his father. I was also very aware that I didn't want to portray James as a totally innocent character.

James's family are very delicately drawn. We see then elliptically, but they're so much more 'present' because of that.
When I wrote the script I wanted the family to seem quite fragmented, so I knew I had to isolate them from each other in some respects. We actually don't see them all together until really quite late in the film. I didn't want to portray them in a caricatured fashion: each of the characters having either good or bad points. It's never black and white who you like and who you don't. I wanted to create a world that was very believable, that you could relate to and also find harsh; find some love there and find some hate there.

I feel that the story is about exploring the death of a soul. It's a question of bad faith. James allows his friend Ryan to die by not acting. On the brink of adulthood, he fails as a moral individual, and that haunts him.
For me it's more about the death of childhood. In the end perhaps it's a metaphorical death – the death of James's spirit. You do meet children who have abandoned hope because of what they've had to deal with. Their destiny is written in their harsh surroundings and they give up.

The ending is about being sucked into that despondent darkness of the canal.
There was a lot of discussion about the ending – which I think is open to interpretation. When I first wrote the film, I didn't want to make it black and white – does he live or die? It was more a sense of things ending, a cycle, a childhood that happened too fast.

Let's discuss the character of Margaret Ann. When we first meet her, she loses her glasses and her world goes out of focus. I found that very moving.
From the first moment you see her, she can hardly see. She is moving around in a slightly blurred world, a world which is quite small. Yet she is still able to love in some respects, even it it's in a

naive way. She is looking for affection in every single little thing, but she is also quite manipulative with the younger James.

James' attempts to retrieve Margaret Ann's glasses neatly nails their unspoken relationship.
It's almost a throwaway thing, but I agree. It says a lot about how he feels about her in that moment.

Do you draw on your background as a photographer in your film-making?
I spent years studying as a photographer, then as a cinematographer, so I got used to watching people all the time, trying to catch the detail that says something about them. What excites me in a film shoot is the unexpected things that happen on the day. Sometimes I like to let things run and see what happens. I work on a very intuitive level; I don't like to over-intellectualize. That's also the way I worked as a photographer.

It seems important for you to let moments breathe.
A lot of people would say that means slow! I guess the way that we have been taught to view things is very bam-bam-bam. A bit of breathing space can give a moment much more power.

The detail where James pulls his mother's laddered tights over her toes says so much about his care for her.
God is in the details. There is a lot of tenderness in the least obvious acts. A minuscule detail like the one you mention can say a lot about a relationship. I am constantly trying to think cinematically. What can be shown instead of said. Sometimes I write dialogue that it is almost superfluous. People rarely say what they mean. I don't often rely on dialogue as the key to a scene. I like to use silence and physical space within a frame to indicate how people are feeling about each other.

You use both professional and non-professional actors. What are you looking for when you're casting?
I am looking for interesting and not obviously beautiful faces. I look for something unpretentious and focused in a person, unselfconsciousness in front of a camera, someone who can internalize rather than externalize their actions. That kind of person is not easy to find. To quote Robert Bresson, I hate 'filmed

theatre'. I choose people who have some similarities to the character I've written and then let it evolve and change. I also think about the dynamics between the actors. Sometimes tension between people can really work in your favour. I find this process really exciting. Ultimately, the challenge is to make the film believable. I'll try any trick in the book to make it happen, even the biggest contrivances. I don't care if I end up looking a complete fool so long as what's up on the screen feels realistic.

How do you work with the children in the cast? Is there much improvisation there?
Some kids are pretty good at improvisation, some not, but the end result can still feel spontaneous. I give the kids lines but they say them in their own way (which is often much better than anything I've written) and with their own timing. If they feel awkward about a line – if they feel they would never say it – we drop it. I don't like doing lots of takes with kids. They get bored. In the case of *Ratcatcher* we had to and it amazed me how consistent many of the kids were. Sometimes I'll let the take run and let them improvise. Other times it's very controlled and close to the script. It's important not to patronize and, conversely, it's important not to manipulate. I'm quite tough with the kids I work with. I always push them and they push me. I think that creates a mutual respect.

How much of the script do you explain to them?
Absolutely nothing, except in special cases. I don't see the point. I don't want to fill their heads with too much stuff which will distract them from what they are doing at that moment. I think this makes it more exciting and spontaneous for them. Each day feels new. I'm not very keen on showing the adult actors the script either. I don't believe you need a history and projection of what is to come to capture a moment of spontaneity. In fact, sometimes I think it can defeat the purpose. Ultimately, a film is made from a series of these moments and these create the story and meaning.

It seems important that you've worked with the same creative team through your shorts to this feature: Alwin Kuchler, Jane Morton, Lucia Zucchetti and producer Gavin Emerson.
As a director you need people around you who you can trust, and who trust you. I work with talented film-makers who understand

the process above and beyond their chosen disciplines. And because we have worked together on all of the films I've made, they understand me very well. We have shorthand which makes everything easier, even in the most stressful situations. We discuss the film early in the script-writing stage. By the time we are shooting, we are all pretty solid on our approach to the material. On *Ratcatcher*, though, I think we would all have appreciated more time in pre-production. For feedback, I also show the script to other film-makers I trust and at least one person who knows nothing about film. I always find this interesting; I am always looking to work with new people who can bring something to the collaboration.

How about the editing of the film? Did the finished item depart very significantly from what had been scripted?

For me a script isn't a book. It is not something to be revered. I think that the *Ratcatcher* script works in its own right and hope that people will enjoy reading it. But to me a script is only a working document, a guide. It is always evolving and changing, and I am happy to scrap things if they don't work, or if I think they will weaken the film as a whole. The more films you make, the more confidence you have to make bold decisions and not be too precious (which is difficult if you've written the film as well).

In terms of influence you mentioned Robert Bresson. I understand that you read his Notes on Cinematography *before you saw any of his films?*

That book was the antithesis of what I was being taught at film school. It was like finding a diamond in the rough. It was great to find something that I identified with just at the time when my ideas about film were evolving. It really became a kind of bible. A few of his films are masterpieces. It is tough cinema for some people, but for me, it's the purest form of cinema. His ideas are so simple but with such integrity behind every single one of them.

There seem to me to be parallels between Ratcatcher *and Bresson's* Mouchette *(1967).*

Mouchette is a great film, but I never like to watch other films when I am making one myself. I try to create a world and go wherever that takes me. Like any other film-maker, I am inspired when I see great cinema – Bergman, Fellini, Cassavettes (there is a long list) – but the postmodern cut-and-paste job, that's just not me. Maybe it's naïve, but I still think you can be original.

CREDITS

Ratcatcher

DAY 1

INT. MRS QUINN'S BEDROOM. DAY

A pair of hands fumbles through the packed contents of a drawer in a cheap teak dressing table.

Fingers rummage through a collection of tatty letters, a string of rosary beads, broken make-up and the framed photo of a man (the estranged Mr Quinn).

One hand searches deeper into the back of the drawer, freezes for an instant, then forcefully pulls out a tiny jeweller's box embossed with cheap gilt lettering.

Reflected in the dressing-table mirror we see Mrs Quinn (early thirties) sitting on top of a double bed. She puts the box in her handbag.

INT. THE QUINNS' LIVING ROOM. DAY

Ryan (eleven years old) stands at the window. He has pulled the yellowing net curtain over his head like a shroud. He spins round and round, cocooning himself in it. The curtain hooks begin to strain on the rail as Ryan trips over his too-long flared trousers and starts to lose his balance.

Mrs Quinn enters the room, walks over to the little Egyptian mummy of curtain and gives it a clout over the head.

RYAN
(whines)
Aoowwww, don't, Ma. Leave me alain.

Ryan begins to unravel himself. He keeps losing his balance and tripping over; the curtain hooks begin to pop off the rail.

MRS QUINN
Aw, fur God's sake, stand still. Look at the state of ma curtain.

3

She bends down and attempts to tuck his trousers into his Wellington boots.

If a've told you once, a've told you umpteen times.

RYAN

Don't, I look like a fanny wae them tucked in.

Ryan stares out of the window, over his mother's head, at a boy (James Gillespie, twelve years old but small for his age) who stands alone on the canal bank, skimming stones across the water.

Mrs Quinn leads Ryan firmly by the jumper and sits him on the sofa.

But I look daft.

MRS QUINN

You'll look dafter when ye trip over and fall oan yer backside.

Mrs Quinn tries to pull off one of his boots. This takes some effort.

RYAN

Awwooohhh, they're too wee, yer hurtin' me. Let me dae it.

She coils the flared trouser around his leg and struggles to pull on the boot again. Ryan pulls away from her.

Ah'll dae it.

MRS QUINN

Suit yerself.

RYAN
(sulks)

They look daft.

EXT. KINTRA STREET. DAY

The sunny street is crowded with playing children. Mrs Quinn and Ryan walk down the pavement. Ryan sulkily lingers behind.

RYAN

Wher are we gone?

MRS QUINN

Go and play – ah'll be back soon.

4

                              RYAN
                          (*surprised*)
      Really?

He eagerly speeds off through a close.

                          MRS QUINN
      Don't go far . . .

INT. CLOSE, KINTRA STREET. DAY

*Framed in the rear doorway of the close is Ryan, crouched down,
tugging his trousers free from his boots. He pelts out of the close and
through the backyard until he is out of sight.*

EXT. PAWNSHOP. DAY

*Through the window of the shop we see Mr Mullen (early fifties) behind
the counter, taking Mrs Quinn's wedding ring from the jeweller's box to
examine it through a watchmaker's magnifier.*

*Mrs Quinn waits eagerly for him to name his price, as he takes a fat roll
of notes from a drawer. He hands her one. She stares at the note,
hesitating before accepting.*

EXT. DUKE STREET CANAL. DAY (HIGH POV)

*Through the yellowing curtain of the Quinns' window, we see James
and Ryan at the edge of the canal. James is pointing at the muddy
shallows as Ryan crouches over, eagerly tucking his trousers back into
his boots.*

EXT. DUKE STREET CANAL. DAY

*Ryan's welly boot sinks deep into the mud. He takes a step forward. His
boots make a squishy sound like a slow, drawn-out fart. James shoves
him. Ryan topples and sits down heavily. James breaks into a fit of
laughter.*

                              RYAN
      Ya bastard!

He struggles up, his backside plastered in mud.

5

JAMES

Huv ye shat yerself, Ryan?

RYAN

Fuck off.

Ryan throws a big globule of mud towards James and hits him smack in the eye with it. He howls with laughter. James is perturbed for a second. Ryan lines up another shot.

JAMES

You're deed.

He lunges at Ryan, felling him again. Ryan struggles to drag James over as well.

A shoving and pulling fight ensues, each boy trying to push the other into the water.

Ryan pins James down, pushing his face under the sludgy surface. James jerks free and lashes out with frantic aggression. He tries to push Ryan over. They grapple.

RYAN

Don't. Ah'm stuck.

Ryan pulls at his leg in an attempt to release it from the deep watery mud. They both topple backwards into the water. Breaking free, James scrabbles through the mud and up the bank, and runs far off down the towpath.

He stops, gasping for breath, and looks back.

The water of the canal is glassy and still. Ryan is nowhere to be seen.

EXT. SHOE SHOP. DAY

Through the window display we see Mrs Quinn take a pair of boy's brown leather sandals to the counter. She pays with a one-pound note.

EXT. KINTRA STREET. DAY

Children weave back and forth across the street, shouting and playing.

In the distance we see Ma (James's mother, Anne Gillespie, early thirties) walking up the street. Her face is flushed and she sways a little with the weight of two full bags of shopping she carries in each hand.

Ma slows and smiles as a neighbour approaches her. They exchange a few words.

Ma continues her journey up the street, getting closer towards us until she passes out of view. We linger on the children playing in the street for a moment.

EXT. FIRHILL BASIN TOWPATH. DAY

James walks along the path.

Two men breathlessly race past him, one a little way in front of the other.

Shouts and screams are heard in the far distance.

James watches the men disappear out of sight.

INT. SECOND LANDING, THE CLOSE, KINTRA STREET. DAY

Ma slowly reaches the top of the second flight of stairs. She stands, statue-like, on the landing, staring out of the window.

Ma's head is framed by the clear blue sky and perfect white clouds outside the window.

The squeals of playing children echo in the close.

INT./EXT. CLOSE/DUKE STREET CANAL. DAY (HIGH POV)

Ma is transfixed by the serene image of a man stretched the whole length of a dinghy, floating in the middle of the canal. Face down, head bowed over the edge, his long hair trails in the black water. His arms are submerged up to the shoulders. His bare back and raw, sunburned shoulders contort as he pulls at something beneath the surface.

The 'boat man' becomes suddenly animated, his face visible as he screams in urgency at a man passing by on the bank. (His cries are near silent, through the thick glass of the window.)

The passer-by struggles to remove his shoes and socks. The boat man shouts to him again. A single shoe is abandoned on the bank as the passer-by wades into the water.

More people come into view and crowd towards the bank. They obscure the dinghy as it moves towards them.

A huddle of men hauls a small body face down from the water and struggle to turn it over.

The small crowd stands in an impotent circle around the prostrate boy.

INT. THE CLOSE, KINTRA STREET. DAY

Ma's arms are straining at the weight of her heavy shopping bags but she does not put them down.

EXT. DUKE STREET CANAL BANK. DAY

Muddy water pours from two wellington boots.

A puddle of wetness seeps from the limp, waterlogged body.

Ryan's white face is clearly visible in the relentless sun.

INT. KITCHEN. DAY

The shopping bags stand on the table. One of the bags rolls over, spilling some of its contents on to the table. We reveal Ma at the kitchen window. The back of her head is framed by the clear blue sky and perfect white clouds outside.

Ma's hands bear deep red imprints across the palms from the shopping-bag handles. She rubs her hands together to soothe them.

Close up we hear the sound of feet pounding up the stone steps of the close. Ma's head turns to the door.

INT. THE CLOSE, KINTRA STREET. DAY

We follow James running up the stairs, framed tight on the back of his head and shoulders as he rounds the corner. We hear the sound of his breathing close up. His own footsteps sound distant.

INT. KITCHEN. DAY

Ma stands stiffly facing the door.

Close up: the sound of heavy footsteps running through the flat.

James speeds in and stops dead at the sight of Ma. She is staring at him, her face a tight mask. Her eyes well up. He stares back, frozen, his breathing shallow. Ma breaks the stillness of the moment and slaps him hard across the face.

He stands shocked, his cheek burning.

She pulls him to her and holds him tight, rocking him slightly, crying. We hold on his expression.

We move round, giving the first clear impression of the space and decor: the fireplace, the big marital bed which is set back in a recess.

FADE TO BLACK.

DAY 2

EXT. KINTRA STREET. DAY

A hearse moves sluggishly up the street, passing families who stand grouped together against the entrances of their respective closes. A few people are leaning out of open windows.

Bags of rubbish are piled at the lampposts and at irregular intervals along the gutters.

The hearse pulls up beside a huddle of men (a few in suits). Among them is Da (George Gillespie, James's father), Boaby (a refuse worker, gangly, early twenties) and Andy (mid-thirties, heavy gut).

The chauffeur (early forties, a pale whippet of a man) opens his door, knocking over a bag of rubbish. He kicks the bags out of the way with his foot. Some of the contents spill out, making the mess worse. He mumbles to himself, cursing. The pallbearer gets out on his side.

ANDY

So that's the boy?

He gestures towards the small coffin in the back of the hearse.

CHAUFFEUR

Yep.

The chauffeur takes a packet of cigarettes from his breast pocket. He offers them around to the men. They all accept and crowd round him for a light.

There is a moment of silence. They all stare into the hearse.

BOABY

Terrible, innit?

The men murmur their agreement.

        (looks skyward)

Still, it's gonny be a nice day fur it, eh?

DA

Fuck sake, Boaby.

There are muffled sniggers among the group. The chauffeur checks his watch.

CHAUFFEUR

Ah better let her know am here. Ave goat two more tae cart aff before three . . .

He takes a long drag of his cigarette and walks towards the close.

        (gestures to the coffin)

Don't let him go anywher, will ye?

He walks into the close, leaving the stunned men with another awkward silence. They stare at the coffin.

Andy produces a small bottle of whisky from his inside pocket and goes to take a swig.

ANDY

God bless the wee cunt.

Andy gulps the whisky and passes the bottle to Da. Kids are making faces through the hearse.

DA

Beat it, yous. Get away from there.

The kids scarper, knocking over some rubbish bags.

Boaby? Ye better move yer arse.

BOABY

Whit?

DA

She'll be coming oot any minute noo.

BOABY

Whit ye oan aboot?

Da winks at Andy, then looks at the piles of rubbish beside the hearse. Andy shakes his head and tut-tuts.

ANDY

Fuck sake, Boaby . . .

He gestures with his head towards the rubbish.

DA

The poor wuman disny want tae see aw that shite lying aboot the day.

BOABY

Whit's it goat tae dae wae me?

ANDY

Well, don't jist stand ther like a big turd, go and move it.

Boaby obediently lollops towards the bags. He stops before he reaches them, coming to his senses.

BOABY

Hi . . . why me?

DA

It's yer joab, innit?

Boaby shrugs and goes to lift the bag. Once his back is turned the others snigger.

ARTIE

(*off-screen*)

Stoap! Ah canny allow ye to dae that, son.

They all look up to a first-floor window. Artie (mid-forties, an overly officious shop steward) is leaning out. Jeers and laughter erupt amid the group.

DA

Go oan, son.

ARTIE
(*authoritarian*)

Do not touch that bag!

ANDY

Don't listen tae that auld fart.

ARTIE

Ah canny let ye dae that, son. You are about tae breach strike
procedure.

ANDY

Aw, fur fuck's sake, Artie, who's gonny know?

ARTIE
(*livid*)

Ah know! They'll be nae blacklegs in ma union.

Artie disappears inside, thudding the window shut.

*Boaby sheepishly goes to move the bags. Artie charges out of the close
(topless with greying chest hair, bare feet, doing up his belt). He grabs at
the bag.*

BOABY

Whit?

Da and Andy are pissing themselves.

*The chauffeur emerges from the close and turns to usher Mrs Quinn on
to the street. The pallbearer follows.*

Da and Andy fall silent.

*Artie wrenches the bag from Boaby, turns to see Mrs Quinn, then
delicately places it away from the hearse.*

*A car arrives and parks in front of the hearse, its engine still running.
The estranged husband, Mr Quinn, waits behind the wheel.*

*The chauffeur slips into the driver's seat. The pallbearer gets into the
passenger seat.*

12

Mrs Quinn waits on the pavement, staring blankly at the small coffin. The men stand awkwardly.

ARTIE

(meaningfully raising his eyes to the heavens)

He's away tae a better place now, hen.

Mrs Quinn doesn't react.

Artie meekly moves the bags away from the side of the hearse.

Mrs Quinn hesitates, then gets in the passenger seat.

The hearse pulls away from the kerb and waits as Mr Quinn U-turns his car. His front wheel mounts the kerb in front of Ma and James's sisters, Anne Marie (aged six) and Ellen (aged fourteen), on the opposite side of the road.

We see James sitting inside a close in semi-darkness, away from the groups of people, his eyes fixed on Mrs Quinn's gloved hands as they rhythmically rub together. The two vehicles trundle slowly up the rise of the road, disappearing up the street.

EXT. ANOTHER STREET. DAY

Moving clouds reflect off an abstraction of shiny black metal. We pull out to reveal the bonnet of the hearse viewed from above, its wheels spinning hypnotically over tarmac with a repetitive rumble.

EXT. DUKE STREET CANAL. DAY

James's blank face is a pale reflection in the black water.

The canal bank is deserted apart from James's stick-like figure standing in the shallows at the scene of Ryan's death.

He tentatively takes a few steps forward into the mud.

He becomes aware of a figure approaching in the distance further along the bank.

The watery mud deepens quickly, rising round his ankles. His face pallid with fear, James tries to move back towards the bank. He is stuck fast. His body jolts as he struggles to release his leg from the tomb of mud. His foot pops out, shoeless; his sock half on. He fishes for his shoe, retrieves it, then scrambles like an insect up the bank.

DAY 3

INT. KITCHEN. MORNING

James is on all fours, feeding a tiny mouse which is caught by the tail in the trap.

Ma squints as she threads a needle. She puts her foot up on the chair beside her and starts to darn a hole in the toe of her stocking. The teapot and a couple of unopened brown envelopes lie on the table.

Off-screen the sound of a front door opening as Da arrives home from work.

DA

(*off-screen*)

Awright, hen.

James scarpers.

Da enters the kitchen carrying an industrial-sized can of paint. He sifts the letters with his free hand, then pushes them to one side.

Still nae word. Maybe there'll be a second post, eh?

MA

Mmmm.

DA

Pete Connelly was two months finding out.

MA

Mmm.

DA

They goat a smashing house.

He sits the huge can of paint on the table in front of Ma.

The work were gonny chuck these oot.

MA

(*looking up*)

Whit that's fur?

14

DA

It's brand new, huvny even been opened.

MA

Whit colour is it?

DA

(*enthusiastic*)

A nice pastel shade.

He prises off the lid with a spoon handle to show her. Ma looks at him, incredulous. She laughs.

MA

You've goat tae be jokin'. It's grey!

DA

No, it's no: it's pale blue.

MA

Och, yer arse it is.

DA

Look at it in the light.

He marches over to the window and studies it.

Aye, it's pale blue . . .

(*unsure*)

Definitely.

MA

(*laughing*)

Your no puttin' that up in here.

She finishes off her stitching and snaps the thread.

DA

Whit's up wae it? That's good-quality paint.

MA

It's bloody horrible!

She steps into her shoes in silence.

DA

I just thought it would brighten the place up a bit, eh?

MA

(*adamant*)

Whit's the point? We're movin'.

DA

Ay, aye, maybe.

Ma gives him the evil eye. She puts her coat on over her overalls.

Da marches back to the paint can and forces the lid on.

(*muttering under his breath*)

Ah canny win.

Ellen staggers into the room in her nightgown, still half asleep. Ma glances at her and nods.

MA

There's tea in the pot if ye want some.

She exits the kitchen.

(*off-screen*)

Aw, fur God's sake!

The front door slams shut.

Da pads out of the kitchen. He returns from the hall with three more huge cans of battleship-grey paint. He carefully stashes them under the bed and then attends to his tea.

EXT. THE OUTSIDE TOILET IN KINTRA STREET BACKYARDS. DAY

The back is blanketed with rubbish bags.

Da holds the squeaking mouse by the tail over the toilet pan. He drops it down and pulls the flush. He turns around to discover Anne Marie watching him close behind. He avoids looking at her troubled expression as he walks back to the close.

Anne Marie stares forlornly into the toilet pan.

Da returns with bags of rubbish and throws them on to the growing mountain. He shouts up towards the open window of a flat.

DA

(*disgusted*)

Fucking strike, the place is turning into a shit-hole.

BOABY

(*off-screen; distant, from inside his flat*)

Piss off.

INT. KITCHEN. DAY

Ellen stands at the ironing board in her vest and skirt hurriedly ironing her blouse.

James sits at the kitchen table, bored. He pours the Saxa salt on the table and makes criss-crossing roads in it with his forefinger.

Ellen puts her blouse on and goes to a big chest of drawers next to Ma and Da's bed. She takes a make-up bag out of the top drawer and sits opposite James at the table. She unzips the bag and fishes in it, taking out a compact mirror and lipstick. She holds the mirror up and carefully applies the crimson lipstick. She catches James staring at her.

ELLEN

Whit ur you lookin at, ya wee pervert?

JAMES

That's Ma's.

ELLEN

Sooo! Ma told me Ah kin use if it Ah like.

She grabs her cotton bag from the floor, slings it over her shoulder and marches towards the kitchen door.

(*without turning to face James*)

Stoap makin' a mess.

She slams the front door on her way out of the flat.

EXT. WINDOW MATCH ON TO KINTRA STREET BACKYARDS. DAY

James hangs out of the kitchen window. He watches Anne Marie staring into the outside toilet.

17

Ellen walks out of the close. James spits, aiming at her head. She doesn't notice as the grog misses her by a couple of inches.

EXT. KINTRA STREET BACKYARDS. DAY

Ellen daintily makes her way through the rubbish in the back, taking care not to dirty her shoes. She gets to the washing line, unpegs her cardigan and puts it on. Off-screen wolf whistles come from the adjacent backyard.

> BOY
> (*off-screen*)

Awright, gorgeous.

Off-screen laughter from a crowd of boys. She ignores them but haughtily and self-consciously makes her way back to the close. James shouts down at her.

> JAMES

Wher ur you gone?

Ellen is taken aback, losing her composure. Her eyes find him at the window. Annoyed, she gives him the V sign. He spits down at her as she enters the close, missing her again.

INT. LIVING ROOM. DAY

James moves quickly through the flat to the living-room window.

EXT. KINTRA STREET. DAY

POV from the Gillespies' living-room window. James watches Ellen walk down the length of the street, then break into a run when a bus passes her. She manages to catch it at the stop.

CUT TO:

INT. LIVING ROOM. DAY

Da enters the living room and switches on the TV: football. He throws himself on to the sofa.

James sits down in an adjacent armchair.

DA

Huv ye no goat a pal or somethin'?

James gets up and skulks past Da towards the door.

Wher ur you gone?

JAMES

Naewhere.

DA

Well, if you're gonny be hinging around here aw day ye kin make yersel useful. Get us a tinny fae the fridge.

James draws him a dirty look.

Whit?

James leaves the room.

INT. KITCHEN. DAY

James opens the fridge door and releases one can of Tennent's from a four-pack, then closes the door.

He throws the can up in the air and catches it as he walks around the kitchen. He shakes it violently, goes to open it, thinks better of it and puts it back in the fridge. He takes out the remaining three cans and shakes two of them violently, quite enjoying himself. He puts the shaken cans back in the fridge.

He pulls the ring pull back on the remaining unshaken can. The lager froths over a little.

Da can be heard in the background getting carried away with the football.

DA
(*off-screen*)

Yess. That's it. Keep the baw ... That's it ... Yes, yes ...

James takes a sup of the beer.

(*off-screen*)

Ya beauty!

Disgusted, James spits it back into the can.

> ANNE MARIE
> (*off-screen*)

Ah saw you.

James turns to see her smug little face behind him.

Ah'm tellin' oan you.

She makes a bolt for the door. James sticks his foot out and she falls flat on her face, bumping her head hard on the floor.

Aaoooowwww!

She looks up at him, shocked for a moment, then her face begins to crumple and big tears well up. James quickly picks her up, cradling her in his arms and tickling her. She is half crying, half laughing. He throws her up and catches her.

> JAMES

Wheeeeeee!

Anne Marie laughs heartily.

> ANNE MARIE

Again.

He accommodates her.

> JAMES

Ther you're a big lassie, eh? You're no gonny greet, ur ye?

She laughs.

> DA
> (*off-screen; annoyed*)

Wher's ma beer?

INT. LIVING ROOM. DAY

James hands Da the can of lager.

> DA

No want tae watch the fitba? It's the Old Firm match.

JAMES

Ah don't like fitba.

He goes to leave the room. Passing Anne Marie, he gives her a silencing look.

ANNE MARIE

Kin Ah watch the fitba, Daddy?

She clambers up on Da.

DA

Mon, hen.

Da pulls her on to the sofa and sits her beside him. Anne Marie presses her forefinger up her nostril.

ANNE MARIE

(*looking smugly to James*)

Ah like fitba.

James leaves the room.

Daddy, is the mouse still in the toilet?

DA

Whit, hen? Mmm, he's away tae the sea . . . C'mon, Lennox . . . That's it . . . C'mon . . . Yes . . .

ANNE MARIE

The seaside?

INT. KITCHEN. DAY

The football from the TV in the living room can be heard in the background.

DA

(*off-screen*)

Aye, that's right, the seaside . . . Oh, naw! Ya bloody idiot.

James hangs out of the kitchen window.

High POV: Kintra Street backyards from Gillespies' kitchen window.

In the next back along James sees Matt Munroe (fifteen years old, a hard expressionless face) and his gang (five other boys aged between fourteen and sixteen – Billy, Tommy, Mackie, Stef and Hammy) running and jumping over the piles of rubbish. Each has a boulder or stick in his hands and they appear to be chasing something between the rubbish bags.

ANNE MARIE
(off-screen)

Daddy, James hurt me.

DA
(off-screen)

Sshhhhh, hen. Watch the game.

Round and round the boys go, laughing and beating their weapons into the soft bags, until they finally unify in the far corner of the back, obscuring James's view.

ANNE MARIE
(off-screen)

James wis drinking your beer.

The gang rains down blows on the object of their chase. Off-screen we hear the sound of the front door closing.

EXT. KINTRA STREET BACKYARDS. DAY

James cuts through the close and through the squashed bags of rubbish which completely cover the back. One of the bags seems to wriggle beneath his feet. He stops to watch; nothing moves. He cuts across to the adjacent backyard. The boys are gone. He makes for the corner they had gathered in, kicking through the rubbish.

He scrambles away up the grassy verge towards the canal.

EXT. THE 'BASIN', DUKE STREET CANAL. DAY

A roar and swell of noise from the football stadium fill the air.

James watches the distant scene of an angler on the bank, his ten-year-old son at his side. Both are very still and silent. Their lines catch the sunlight.

The angler gently reels in his line, then faster and more excitedly. The son crouches down and props his rod on the bank. He lifts up the landing net and works with his father to land the fish. James catches a glimpse of a quivering fin as they lay the net on the grass. They crouch over their catch.

James approaches tentatively.

ANGLER

No bad, eh? It's about three or four pounds, a wee beauty.

James is now alongside them, staring with fascination at the prehistoric-looking fish. Its body is brown, about a foot long, with vermilion fins. It curls frantically, then lies still, gasping.

The son goes to take the hook from its mouth.

No, son, careful, no. Ah'll dae that. See its teeth, ye kin get a nasty bite fae thim, but it's really the fins and the gills ye huv goat tae avoid. See them –
        (*he points to two separated dorsal fins*)
– the front one, razor-sharp spines. Fourteen a thim –
(*he demonstrates by spreading the fin apart with the tip of his rod*)
– gee ye a right nasty cut.

JAMES

Whit is it, mister?

ANGLER
(*looks to his son*)

Whit is it?

SON

A perch?

ANGLER

That's right.

JAMES

Dae ye eat it?

ANGLER
(*laughing*)
It wid eat you given half a chance.

The angler skilfully unhooks the still-breathing fish. His son dips the net back into the water and the perch darts off. James watches with fascination as the angler's son selects two maggots from the bait box and hands one to his father. They both hook the bait and elegantly cast their lines back into the water.

JAMES

Look, there's one. Ah saw one.

He points enthusiastically.

ANGLER

Watch yer shadow, son. If they see yer shadow, it scares them aff.

In the background noisy football supporters from the winning team begin to filter on to the bank from the stadium.

JAMES

Kin they hear them shouting?

SON

They don't hear anything above the water.

Football fans walk past them on the towpath.

SMART-ARSE SUPPORTER

Plenty of salt an' vinegar wae mine. Cheers, mate.

James and the anglers ignore the stupid comments and stare intently at the bobbing floats.

Off-screen there is an almighty splash.

James looks in the direction of the noise. Pause. A man's head surfaces in the middle of the canal.

GORDIE

Mon in, the water's fucking brilliant ... It's warm.

A few drunken fans further along the bank strip their tops and shoes off and dive-bomb into the canal, cheered on by others.

ANGLER

Bloody idiots. Mon, son, reel yer line in. We're no gonny catch anything now.

They hurry to dismantle their rods. James seals the bait box up and goes to hand it to the angler's son.

SON

It goes in there.

He points to a small rucksack.

Gordie shows off, sculling back and forth in the deep water, singing a 'bigot' song.

GORDIE

Oh, no Pope of Rome, no chapels tae sadden my eyes, no nuns and no priests, fuck yer rosary beads, every day is the twelfth of July . . .

Tam, a fan of the beaten team, shouts to Gordie from the bank.

TAM

Aye, you'll no sing so loud when you git oot ay ther, ya cunt!

GORDIE

Whit ye waitin' fur, then? C'mon, ya bass.

Tam lunges head-first into the water, screaming a demented and unintelligible battle cry, and swims a rapid crawl towards Gordie. Several of Tam's mates follow him in like lemmings.

The angler and his son leave.

MACKIE

Kill the bastard, Tam!

Water erupts in slow motion as Tam rains blows on to an opposition supporter standing in the shallows. James watches, transfixed by the violence.

Right in front of James another man clambers up the bank and out of the water. He glares right at James, then staggers past him, blind drunk. James turns to see that the man's shoulders are gashed and blood is running down his bare back. James stares as the man weaves unsteadily through the dispersing crowd.

Supporters laugh at the state he's in.

PASSING SUPPORTER

Ye better go an' get that looked at, mate. That's nasty.

The man glares at the supporter, staggers back a little, then stumbles off.

James makes his way through a group of oncoming fans. A man passing thrusts a can of lager at him.

SPAM

In a oner, like the team dae it.

Spam gives an example by downing his whole can of lager in one go. James follows, less eloquently. Half the can spills all over him. He almost retches.

WULLIE

Your awright, wee man.

Wullie laughs heartily as he thuds the coughing James hard on the back, almost knocking the stuffing out of him. Wullie crouches down.

Mon up oan ma shoulders.

James reluctantly climbs on to Wullie's shoulders.

Mon, ye can be the team's mascot, eh?

James towers above everyone, looking shit-scared, on Wullie's shoulders.

They all head off along the bank singing.

WULLIE AND HIS MATES
(*in unison*)

Well it's a grand auld team to play for. Well it's a grand auld team to get the jail for . . .

James sways precariously on Wullie's shoulders.

EXT. KINTRA STREET BACKYARDS. DAY

James sits on a broken wall at the far side of the backs, looking pale and nursing a can of lager procured from the football supporters. He faces on to the backyards of the tenements.

A narrow pathway from the toilet to the rear entrance of the close is the only clearing in a sea of rubbish bags.

Three of Matt Munroe's gang are loitering around the outside toilet, obscuring James's view through the door.

A moment later Matt Munroe bursts out of the toilet, followed by Billy, Tommy and Margaret Anne.

MARGARET ANNE

Gie me them back, ya bastard.

The group of boys chorus laughter.

TOMMY

Look it the stupit cow. She canny see a thing.

BILLY

Huv ye lost yer knickers as well, Margaret Anne?

MARGARET ANNE

Fuck off.

She clumsily takes a swipe, missing him by a long shot. Billy laughs and dances swiftly around her. Margaret Anne lashes out but manages to miss Billy every time.

BILLY

Kin ye see me, Margaret Anne? Look, Ah'm here. Och, yer too slow, hen.

TOMMY

Och, leave the poor cow alain.

Billy pecks Margaret Anne on the cheek. As he dodges Margaret Anne's grip he pulls up her skirt.

Margaret Anne tries to follow him, but she moves clumsily and slowly, as if disorientated.

James climbs up the verge beyond the wall. Clutching his stomach, in sickness, he unsteadily disappears over the horizon.

EXT. DUKE STREET CANAL. DAY

James sits on the low wall of the towpath doubled up.

Matt and his gang appear on the towpath, slowly followed by Margaret Anne.

Matt throws something into the canal near James, then sprints off along the towpath followed by the other boys.

BILLY

See ye next time, darlin'.

Margaret Anne doesn't notice James until she is quite close. She leans on the wall beside him.

MARGARET ANNE

Kin ye see my glasses?

James lowers himself from the wall, crosses the towpath and bends forward at the water's edge.

We see the glasses caught in a bare spring mattress under the yellowish water.

Kin ye see thim?

JAMES
(*weakly*)

Naw.

Margaret Anne sits on the wall. She fumbles in her pocket and produces a packet of Regal Kingsize cigarettes and a box of matches. She pauses to itch her scalp then lights up a fag.

James is motionless, still bent double at the water's edge.

MARGARET ANNE

Kin ye see thim? Ur you awright? C'mere.

James slowly approaches her. She smiles at him. He climbs on to the wall and sits beside her, stupefied.

Thanks fur lookin' anyhow. Whit's your name?

JAMES

James.

There is a pause. They both stare off into the canal. She takes a long drag on her cigarette and plays with a pebble from the wall. She attempts to throw it into the water. It's a pathetic attempt and the stone lands on the towpath.

MARGARET ANNE

Did you know that boy who drooned doon here?

JAMES
(*mumbled*)

Naw.

Margaret Anne runs her fingers through her tangled hair and scratches violently at the nape of her neck.

James stares at a scab on her knee, a drop of blood congealing where it has cracked. They sit in silence for a moment.

MARGARET ANNE

Do you want to touch it?

Misinterpreting where he has been looking, Margaret Anne takes his limp hand and rests it on her thigh.

James's head rolls loosely forward like a doll's and he vomits on to the ground. Margaret Anne strokes the hand still resting on her knee.

(*whispered*)
Don't worry, wee man. You'll be awright.

EXT. DUKE STREET CANAL BANK. LATE AFTERNOON/EARLY
EVENING

The water surface ripples. We reveal James face down on the bank, leaning over the water with a stick.

EXT. KINTRA STREET BACKYARDS. NIGHT

James is walking back home. He freezes as he sees the ghost-like figure of Mrs Quinn standing motionless, staring into nothingness. We stay on the transfixed figure as James moves out of view.

INT. CHILDREN'S BEDROOM. NIGHT

Ellen and Anne Marie lie in the darkness together in a small double bed. Anne Marie is asleep and sprawled out, taking up the majority of the space of the mattress, with most of the covers bunched up around her. Ellen is awake and trying to extract them by loosening Anne Marie's tight little fists from around the blankets. She loses patience and forcefully grabs them. Anne Marie half stirs. Mumbling and whining, she kicks out at Ellen.

Off-screen the sound of James's footsteps pounding up the stairs.

INT. KITCHEN. NIGHT

Ma lies uncannily still, her mouth a little open, on top of the big bed. She is fully clothed in her nylon overall.

James stands transfixed at the foot of the bed. Ma looks dead.

He touches her big toe, which peeps through a small hole in her tights. She flinches but doesn't wake.

James walks to the window.

EXT. PATH BEHIND THE WALL AT KINTRA STREET BACKYARDS. NIGHT

POV: from Gillespies' kitchen window.

A rat darts along the wall.

Da and Rita (late thirties, mutton dressed as lamb) stop on the path beyond the wall of the backyards.

                              DA
That's me.

                            RITA
                          (*drunken*)
Yer no gonny let me walk up the rest ay this dark path oan
ma oan, ur ye?
            (*she clumsily puts her arms around Da's neck*)
Aw, don't go jist yet. Why don't ye come up tae ma place fur
a wee . . . coffee?

She cackles. Da laughs with her while at the same time attempting to push her away.

EXT. BEYOND THE WALL OF KINTRA STREET BACKYARDS. NIGHT

Ground level.

DA

(*trying to prise Rita's arms off him*)

Ah'd better go, she'll be waitin'.

RITA

(*shouts for all to hear*)

Whit you need is a real wuman tae take care ay ye …

A loud rap on a window-pane cuts through her voice. Da shushes her.

Whit the fuck wis that?

They both look up, searching for the direction of the noise.

INT./EXT. VIEW FROM GILLESPIES' KITCHEN WINDOW. NIGHT

From the window of the Gillespies' kitchen we see Da and Rita on the path beyond the backs, looking around in surprise. James is ducked out of sight and crouching below the sill.

INT. GILLESPIES' KITCHEN. NIGHT

Ma turns on the bed without stirring.

Off-screen Da noisily enters the darkened flat.

James scarpers. He stumbles into the kitchen and kneels down on the floor, almost falling flat on his face. He takes a mousetrap from his coat pocket and, after some initial problems working it out, eventually sets it.

INT. CHILDREN'S BEDROOM. NIGHT

Ellen rolls Anne Marie on to her belly with a shove and turns her back to her. Snuggling up in the blankets, she closes her eyes. Anne Marie's leg hangs over the edge of the bed, the sole of her grubby and black foot almost touching the floor.

There is a scampering sound and a rhythmic light scratching from under the bed. Ellen stares fixedly into the dark corner of the room. She draws the covers tight around her neck, leaving Anne Marie half covered.

James's single bed is empty.

DAY 4

James is standing at the water's edge.

He stares at the objects caught in the algae blanket on the surface of the black water. Plastic bags float like ghosts. A burst football is caught, immobile, in the brilliant-green surface.

Behind James, Kenny (ten years old) runs awkwardly, with his hands in his pockets, almost losing his balance. He slows down at James's side.

> KENNY
> *(out of breath)*
Want tae see what Ah've got?

James ignores him.

Look.

Kenny fishes in his pocket.

Look!

Kenny opens his hand.

> JAMES
Ah don't see anything?

Kenny's hand is empty. He contorts in a fit of giggles with both arms up one sleeve of his coat, forming a straitjacket.

> KENNY
Don't, you're ticklin' me!

He drags a plump hamster from the depths of his sleeve and holds her by the tail for James to see.

James takes it gently in his palm and strokes its back.

> JAMES
Whit's its name?

> KENNY
Suzy, it's a she.

JAMES

It's nice.

KENNY
(*ranting eagerly*)
Ah've got a gerbil and all and a budgie and my ma says she's
gonny get me a mouse for ma birthday and fur ma next
birthday Ah'm gonny get a cat and a dog, and fur the
birthday after that Ah'm gonny get a pony, and for the
birthday after that Ah'm gonny get a lion . . .

JAMES
(*interrupts*)
That's nice, Kenny.

*He hands Kenny back the hamster. Kenny drops it in his pocket. James
bends down and picks up a stick from the bank.*

KENNY
Look! Ah'm a member of the RSPCA.
(*he shows James the badge on his duffel coat*)
My ma says Ah'm gonny huv the biggest giantest zoo in the
world when Ah grow up.

JAMES
(*uninterested*)
Is that right?

James idly pokes the stick into the canal.

KENNY
Whit ye looking fur?

JAMES
Nothin'.

KENNY
Ther's wee fishes in ther, minnows an' sticklebacks.

JAMES
Huv ye ever seen a perch?

                    KENNY
                (*eyes light up*)

A per ... sh?

                    JAMES

Aye.

                    KENNY

Is it a fish?

                    JAMES

It's aboot that size.
                (*he gestures the length, exaggerating*)
Way big orange spiky fins thit kin cut ye tae pieces, an'
millions of wee spiky teeth.

                    KENNY
                (*awed*)

Huv you caught wan?

                    JAMES

Ah saw a guy fishing up here the other day. He caught a
beauty?

                    KENNY
                (*excited*)

Ah want tae catch wan.
                (*he studies the canal*)
Ah've goat a net. Want tae try an' catch wan?

                    JAMES

It's no that easy.

Kenny studies the canal for a moment, deep in thought.

                    KENNY

A persh.

                    JAMES

See ye later, eh?

He turns to walk away.

                    KENNY

Whit am Ah, James?

                     34

Kenny runs in front of James, arms outstretched like an aeroplane, down the grassy verge and away from the canal bank towards the backs of the houses.

James looks bewildered for a moment.

> (*excited*)
> Ah'm a bird, Ah'm a bird, Ah'm an ostrich. Ostrich canny fly.
> (*he flaps into the distance, shouting*)
> You should come up the morra and see ma zoo!

His voice fades into the distance.

EXT. KINTRA STREET. DAY

Rubbish bags piled at lamp-posts dot the pavement and gutters. A man in a sombre suit makes his way up the street. He is red and sweating in the sunshine. He pauses to wipe his brow, tucking his briefcase under his arm.

INT. HALLWAY/CLOSE, KINTRA STREET. DAY

Anne Marie opens the front door. She looks up at the besuited man.

> INSURANCE MAN
> Is yer mammy ther, hen?

Anne Marie pauses to think of her answer. She shakes her head.

> (*sighs*)
> But Ah saw her oan her way hame from work.

> ANNE MARIE
> She hid tae go oot.

She closes the door so just one eye peeps through.

> (*distraught*)
> My auntie's . . .

> (*she pauses to think*)
> no well.
> (*her voice drops to an almost imperceptible whisper, her eyes drop to her feet*)
> Hospital.

INSURANCE MAN

Ah'm sorry, hen.

Anne Marie goes to close the door.

Hang oan a wee minute, hen. Kin ye make sure yer ma gets
this?

He hands her a card: 'Providence Insurance'.

INT. KITCHEN. DAY

*Da lies asleep on top of the big bed. Ma is crouched with her hands over
her ears.*

Anne Marie enters the room.

MA
(*whispered*)

Has he gone yet?

Anne Marie nods.

Ma makes Anne Marie a 'piece and jam' and hands it to her.

EXT. KINTRA BACKYARDS. DAY

Anne Marie turns on the spot, eating her sandwich.

*Two men scavenge through the rubbish a few backs further along,
separating items of interest or a little value.*

*One pulls a black dead dog from inside a bag. He holds it up by the leg
to inspect it.*

MAN

Look, somebody's chucked out a perfectly good dug.

Both men laugh.

EXT. KINTRA STREET. DAY

*Rubbish bags border the pavement and gutters and crowd in mounds
around lamp-posts.*

Ma walks up the street carrying two plastic bags of shopping. James trails a little way behind her, another bag of Ma's shopping slung over his shoulder.

Mr Quinn's baker's van is parked outside Mrs Quinn's tenement with its back doors open. Boxes and small items of furniture sit on the pavement next to it.

Mr Quinn emerges from the close carrying one end of a huge wardrobe. He is slowly followed by Mrs Quinn, who is struggling with the weight of the other end.

They prop the wardrobe up against the back of the van.

Mr Quinn disappears inside the van and begins hauling one end of it into the back. Mrs Quinn stays outside on the road, trying to push the wardrobe in from the other end.

MR QUINN

Aw, fur God's sake, woman, push ... Push.

MRS QUINN

It's too heavy.

MR QUINN

Put yer back intae it.

There is a lot of mumbled cursing from Mr Quinn. The van shakes visibly. Mrs Quinn is pushing with all her might but the thing won't budge.

She gives up. The wardrobe slides out of the van and crashes to the ground.

Aw, fur fuck sake, Berni.

Mrs Quinn stands staring at the broken wardrobe. She bursts into hysterics.

MRS QUINN

It's your fault. It's aw your fault. It's your fault.

She starts sobbing uncontrollably. Mr Quinn jumps out of the back of the van. He tries to put his arms around her to console her. Mrs Quinn flails her arms at him.

(screaming)

Fuck off. Leave me alain, ya bastard. Leave me.

Mr Quinn backs away from her. Mrs Quinn slumps down on the pavement, her head in her hands.

Ma crosses the street, James hangs back.

Mr Quinn leaves his wife and goes back inside the close.

Ma sits next to Mrs Quinn on the pavement. She takes a cigarette from her overalls and offers her one. Mrs Quinn takes it with a shaky hand. Ma puts an arm around her.

MA

There, you're awright, hen. Don't you worry aboot anything.

MRS QUINN

Ah hate him. Ah hate him. He killed him. It wis him.

MA

Sshhhhhh. Calm doon, hen. Jist calm doon.

Ma rocks Mrs Quinn a little.

MRS QUINN

(screams at the top of her voice)

You killed ma boy.

James, who thinks Mrs Quinn is shouting directly at him, is rooted to the spot. He suddenly breaks into a run, leaving the shopping bags on the pavement.

Wher's wee James gone?

MA

(shouts)

James . . . James!

James freezes and slowly crosses the street to Ma and Mrs Quinn.

MRS QUINN

Wher are ye gone?

JAMES

Nowhere.

MA

Go an' pick up ma bags, you.

Relieved to get away, James bolts across the street and picks up the bags.

MRS QUINN

C'mere back here a minute, son.

JAMES
(*mumbles into his jumper*)
Ah'd better take the bags up.

He heads towards the close.

MA

Dae whit yer telt, you.

MRS QUINN

C'mere. Ah've goat something fur ye.

James reluctantly crosses the street to Mrs Quinn. As he nears her, she violently pulls him towards her chest and holds him tight. His face squashes into the material of her dress.

JAMES
(*terrified, mumbling*)
It wisny ma fault, honest. Ah didny mean it . . .

Mrs Quinn pushes him back, holding him by the arms, and examines him, pushing his fringe from his face.

MRS QUINN

He's gettin' tae be a right good-lookin' boy, isn't he?

She turns to Ma, then back to James.

Yer the double of ma Ryan. The same eyes, don't ye think?

MA
(*uncomfortable*)
A wee bit, mibby.

MRS QUINN

Aye, yer the spittin' image.

James struggles from her grip.

Ah want ye tae go upstairs and bring doon the wee box fae the top of the bed.

James stands fixed to the spot.

MA

Go oan then, dae wit yer telt.

James runs into the close and races up the stairs. He bumps into Mr Quinn, whose face is obscured by the tower of boxes he carries. The boxes fall around them; knives and forks clatter down the stairs.

MR QUINN

Shit.

James avoids his glowering stare and races past him up the stairs.

INT. MRS QUINN'S KITCHEN. DAY

James wanders into the vacant room. There are a few boxes and papers on the floor and clean squares on the wall where pictures once hung. Rat poison is dotted close to the skirting boards. The room has a feeling of desolation about it. An old stained mattress is propped against the wall but otherwise he sees no bed.

He leaves the room.

INT. RYAN'S BEDROOM. DAY

James stands in the doorway. There is a small single bed in the room with many boxes on top of it.

In the far corner hangs a torn 'Bobby Lennox' poster and a solitary Airfix airplane with a broken wing.

He takes the smallest box from the top of the pile and quickly leaves the room.

EXT. KINTRA STREET. DAY

James hands Mrs Quinn the box.

MRS QUINN

Ah hope they'll fit him.

Mrs Quinn hands Ma the box. She opens it. Inside are Ryan's unworn sandals.

> MA
>
> Aw, they're gorgeous. I canny accept ... Let me gee ye something fur them.

> MRS QUINN
>
> Ah don't want anything. Huv them.

> MA
>
> That's awfy good of ye. He needs a new pair as well. I don't know how he did it, but he managed to lose one of his good ones the other day.

> MRS QUINN
>
> I'd rather somedy goat the wear oot of them.

> MA
> *(to James)*
>
> C'mere, you ... Try them on.

> JAMES
>
> I don't want them.

Ma draws him a filthy look. She grabs him by the arm and sits him in between her and Mrs Quinn. James reluctantly puts the shoes on.

They're too wee.

Ma presses the toes of the sandals.

> MA
>
> Oh, stop your moaning, they're a good fit. Stand up and let us see them.

James stands like a cripple.

> MRS QUINN
>
> They suit him.

> MA
>
> Aye, they're lovely. Thanks very much.
> *(to James)*
>
> What do you say?

JAMES

They're too wee.

MA

Thank Mrs Quinn, you ungrateful wee so-and-so.

James stares at his feet.

JAMES

Thanks.

EXT. KINTRA BACKYARDS. LATE AFTERNOON

The rubbish has piled up into mounds, leaving only a clearing in the centre of the concrete surface of the back. James is sat there, hacking at his sandals with a piece of broken glass.

Off-screen the distant sound of a woman screaming from a flat inside one of the tenement buildings.

WOMAN
(*off-screen*)
There's a bloody rat in here ... Kill it, kill it.

EXT. CANAL. EARLY EVE

The water surface ripples. We reveal James face-down on the back, leaning over the water with a stick.

A bloated mass of matted fur floats a little way out on the surface of the water. He tries in vain to hook it with the stick.

The stiff body rolls, revealing the bared teeth and outstretched claws of a dead rat. The body bobs further out of his reach.

James, viewed from behind, hobbles along the towpath, using the stick as a makeshift walkingstick. He lobs the stick into the water and disappears down the slope towards the tenements.

DAY 5

EXT. KINTRA STREET. DAY

James sits alone on the front step of the close facing on to the street. Ellen and Anne Marie pass him. James flicks a 'V' at Ellen's back. Anne Marie sees him do it. She tugs at Ellen's sleeve.

ELLEN

Leave me. What?

ANNE MARIE

He stuck his two fingers up at you.

ELLEN
(*without looking back*)

Tit.

Kids play on the pavement. A few mothers watch them from the close steps. Ellen leaves Anne Marie with two little girls and their mum a few doors down.

James watches her wait at the bus stop.

EXT. BUS STOP AT THE END OF KINTRA STREET. DAY

Ellen stands waiting at the request stop. James sidles up to her and sits on the step of the adjacent close.

JAMES

Where are you going?

ELLEN

Piss off. I'm telling Ma.

JAMES

I can do what I like, it's a free country.

ELLEN

You're not coming with me, no way. Go home.

JAMES

Look at the state of your knees, they're filthy.

Red-faced, she ignores him but she spits saliva into her palms and attempts to wipe her knees clean.

The number 61 bus arrives. Ellen gets on.

James watches the bus round the corner of the street.

43

INT. GILLESPIES' KITCHEN. DAY

James stares at Da sleeping. His Father grunts and turns over. The rhythm of his snoring returns.

Keeping his gaze fixed on him, James reaches into the pocket of Da's trousers on the back of a kitchen chair.

He counts out loose coppers.

INT./EXT. BUS STOP, KINTRA STREET. DAY

James waits on the pavement. Margaret Anne is walking up the opposite side of the street. James watches her. She doesn't see him. The number 61 pulls up.

James counts the pennies into the impatient bus driver's hand.

> BUS DRIVER

Wher tae, son?

> JAMES

Ten pence, please.

> BUS DRIVER
> (*patronizing*)

Whit's yer destination?

> JAMES
> (*mumbled*)

Ten pence, please.

> BUS DRIVER

Dae ye know wher ye're goin', son?

James avoids eye contact; he studies the pennies in the driver's open palm. The bus driver lets out a long sigh and hands James a ticket, gesturing him to move on. The bus moves off from the stop.

INT./EXT. TOP DECK OF THE BUS. DAY

James is upstairs on the front seat of the moving bus. The landscape outside the window gradually transforms from urban streets to hedgerows and open countryside. The piles of rubbish that litter the roadside thin out, then disappear.

EXT. JACQUELINE'S HOUSE, BACK GARDEN. DAY

Ellen and Jacqueline Connolly (aged fourteen) lie on their backs on towels, sunbathing. Jacqueline has a proper swimsuit on. Ellen wears her vest, with her skirt pulled up to her thighs.

Mrs Connolly (mid-thirties) sits on a deck-chair near by.

> ELLEN

Ma ma and da are gonny move here as well.

Mrs Connolly nods her head half-heartedly, giving her a 'we'll see' kind of look.

> (stresses)

We are.

Through the slats of the garden fence she stares out on to a golden wheat field bathed in sunlight.

INT./EXT. BUS PARKED AT TERMINUS. DAY

The bus is empty and stationary, its engine still running. The driver stretches his newspaper across the steering wheel and crouches over to read it. As he turns the page, he catches a glimpse of the top deck in his periscope mirror. James sits quietly waiting upstairs.

> BUS DRIVER
> (shouts)

Right, son, that's us. The end of the line.

James doesn't quite know what to do or if it's him being addressed. He doesn't move.

The Driver's feet pound up the stairs.

> BUS DRIVER

Mon, son. Ur ye gettin' off, ur whit?

The driver pounds back down the stairs. James slowly rises from his seat. He passes the driver having a smoke outside the bus. The driver shakes his head to himself and takes a long drag of his cigarette.

EXT. A ROW OF HOUSES, EASTERHOUSE. DAY

James walks down a concrete path between two rows of the smart new houses. Washing on lines sways slowly outside one row in the brilliant sunshine.

The other row is half built, the houses skeletal, without doors or glass in the window frames. The concrete path ends abruptly at a small, empty building site.

No one is around. James walks tentatively into the last empty house of the row.

INT. EMPTY HOUSE. DAY

James passes through a darkened hall and approaches a small toilet without a door. Inside is a bright new sink and toilet pan. He walks past and climbs a set of stairs without a banister.

Upstairs, he passes more rooms without doors. He enters one, a large whitewashed square. His hand traces the walls.

He enters the bathroom, which contains a big new bath, sink and toilet pan. He pees down the dry toilet. The pee emerges at the base of the pan, creating a damp creeping pattern in the concrete floor. He turns the 'H' tap of the bath. No water comes out. He climbs in and stretches himself right out.

He quietly steps back down the stairs and enters the room at the end of the hallway, a kitchen with two large windows and fitted cupboards covered in plastic.

Outside, a golden wheat field bathed in sunlight sways in a light breeze. James stands awed by the open landscape framed like a painting by the rectangular window.

He climbs on to the sill and sits in silhouette against the bright vista.

He abruptly jumps down to the outside of the building out of view. A moment passes.

He reappears in the distance, running through the field.

EXT. SUMMERSTON FIELD. LATE AFTERNOON

James dives and tumbles through the wheat.

He lies down and blankets his body with the long stems. He blinks up at the clear blue sky.

Off-screen boys voices are heard in the distance.

James turns on to his belly, taking care not to disturb the stems of wheat. Through the long stalks he spies a group of boys passing close by on the path to the river.

EXT. RIVER BANK, SUMMERSTON. LATE AFTERNOON

James sits on the bank, watching the adolescent boys: back-lit shapes treading water in the middle of the river. One boy strips to his underpants and bombs in from the bank. The boys move round each other in the water, laughing and splashing.

EXT. BLACKHILL ROAD. LATE AFTERNOON

Stripped to the waist, James kicks a crushed cola can along the empty pavement.

The number 61 bus thunders past.

EXT. KINTRA BACKYARDS. LATE AFTERNOON/EARLY EVENING

James cuts through an S-shaped path in the mounting piles of black bags. A rat darts out of a bag right in front of him. James stands stock still. The rat makes a beeline for the entrance of the close, fast as lightning. James kicks the bag, another rat darts in his direction. Surprised, James steps back. The rat disappears among the rubbish. James slowly edges forward, hyper-aware and scanning the bags for movement.

> BILLY
> Whit ye up tae, wee man?

James looks up, startled. Billy towers above him, standing on top of the concrete wall which divides the backyard.

                              JAMES

Nothin'.

                              TOMMY

Want tae come wae us?

                              JAMES

Ah dunno ... wher ur ye gone?

                              BILLY

Mon, pal, you kin keep the edgy fur us.

EXT. CANAL TOWPATH. EARLY EVENING

*Matt Munroe, Billy, Tommy and James wander up the towpath
towards the high flats in the near distance. Matt and Billy kid about,
Matt trying to push Billy in the water.*

                              MATT
                            (*laughing*)
Fancy a swim? Fancy a Ryan Quinn?

Billy laughs and pushes him off.

                              BILLY

Fuck off! You first, mate.

Matt stops and turns to face James.

                              MATT

Dae you like swimming?

James shrugs his shoulders.

Are you a good swimmer?

James shrugs his shoulders.

Ah bet ye are. Go on then, dive in.

                              JAMES

Piss off.

*As James tries to edge away from the canal, Matt and Billy sidestep to
block him. Billy grabs James's arms from behind and Matt grabs his
legs. They swing him out over the edge.*

                               48

BILLY AND MATT

One, two, three . . .

TOMMY

Och, leave him alain, that's shite.

Billy and Matt laugh and set James down on the bank.

MATT

Only joking.

James looks serious.

They continue walking down the bank. James hangs back with Tommy.

TOMMY

Don't worry aboot them, they're just trying tae wind ye up.

INT. KITCHEN, MARGARET ANNE'S HIGH-RISE FLAT. EARLY EVENING

A small kitchen leading on to the living room. A cheesy romantic record plays in the background. Matt Munroe stands in the doorway.

MATT

Keep the edgy fae that window in case her ma comes back.

He leads James to the window and ducks out of the room. Tommy assumes a slouched position against the door frame, looking into the living room.

TOMMY

Awright, Margaret Anne. Guess who?

MARGARET ANNE
(*off-screen*)

Billy?

Off-screen laughter from all the boys.

BILLY
(*off-screen*)

Try harder . . . Who is it, Margaret Anne?

MARGARET ANNE
(*off-screen*)

Steven?

Off-screen laughter.

(*off-screen*)
Och, Ah don't know. You better get ma glasses back, ya
prick.

TOMMY
(*mock terror*)

Whooaaaa.

Unable to see into the room, James is watching Tommy.

(*to James*)
Awright ther, wee man?

*James turns back to the window. There is a good view of the snaking
canal. He concentrates on the figure of a man and his dog walking
along the canal bank.*

*Behind James, Billy (doing up his fly) swaps position at the door with
Tommy. James continues to stare out of the window.*

MATT
(*off-screen*)
Who is it, Margaret Anne?

MARGARET ANNE
(*off-screen*)

Tommy?

MATT
(*off-screen*)
Not bad, hen. One out of four.

Off-screen laughter.

The canal towpath is deserted.

BILLY
(*off-screen*)
Hi, Jamie. It's your turn.

James turns to face him.

No want a shot?

Billy beckons James into the room with a motion of his head.

INT. LIVING ROOM, MARGARET ANNE'S HIGH-RISE FLAT. EARLY
EVENING

*Billy and Steven sit in two armchairs facing the sofa. Tommy hangs
back at the kitchen doorway. Matt leans against the wall smoking a
cigarette.*

*Margaret Anne lies passively on the sofa. Her skirt is hitched up to her
thighs, her blouse open, exposing one of her breasts. Her eyes stare
upwards, unfocused, as she unconsciously works her fingernails over her
scalp.*

*James slowly and quietly walks over to the sofa and awkwardly lies on
top of her, his arms kept stiffly at his sides.*

Off-screen sniggers.

TOMMY

Shhhhh!

*James's head rests like a baby's on Margaret Anne's breast. He closes
his eyes.*

INT. LIVING ROOM, MARGARET ANNE'S HIGH-RISE FLAT.
EVENING

Later: we see Margaret Anne and James on the sofa from above.

The gang are gone.

INT. GILLESPIES' LIVING ROOM. NIGHT

*Ma and Da sit together on the white leatherette sofa. Anne Marie sits
trance-like on the carpet in front of the black-and-white TV set
watching* Tom Jones Live from Las Vegas.

James is slumped on an armchair behind her. He kicks off his shoes.

Da is drunk.

DA
(*slurred*)
Ye know Ah love you, don't ye, hen?

Anne Marie turns to face them.

MA
(*laughs*)
Och, away ye go, you.

DA
C'mere, gorgeous.

He pulls Ma towards him and gives her a kiss on the cheek.

MA
(*smiling*)
Aye, Ah'm always gorgeous when yer half cut.

Da slumps back on the sofa. Ma continues watching TV. Da notices Anne Marie is watching them.

DA
She's a great wuman. One in a million, eh?

Ma rolls her eyes in a 'What's he like?' manner. Anne Marie turns back to the frenzied rendition of 'What's New, Pussycat'.

James stares loathingly at Da, who is falling asleep.

Da's head tips back over the edge of the sofa with his mouth open, catching flies.

DAY 6

INT. LIVING ROOM. DAY

James is slouched on the white leatherette sofa watching a Tom and Jerry cartoon. He scratches his scalp vigorously and unconsciously.

DA
(*off-screen*)
James!

JAMES
(*annoyed*)

Whit?

DA
(*off-screen*)

Ur ma fags in ther?

JAMES

Naw!

Da marches into the room.

DA

Aw fur . . . Ah bet ye huvny even looked, ya lazy wee swine.

Da starts pulling up the cushions.

Get up. They must be under ye.

James looks underneath himself.

JAMES

Ther no here.

Da looks down the side of the sofa, then to the back of the TV, blocking James's view. He switches it over to the football results.

Ah wis watchin' that!

Da ignores him, engrossed by the TV. He tucks his shirt in and does up his belt. James stares at clumps of shaving foam that have escaped Da's notice behind his ears and the dots of paper on his cheek.

You pong.

Da doesn't hear him.

DA

Whit?

James gets up and leaves the room.

INT. KITCHEN. DAY

On the kitchen table a bottle of Prioderm lotion, a bowl of water and a bar of carbolic soap stand on a sheet of newspaper.

53

Ma is scrubbing Anne Marie's head with the carbolic soap.

James pads in unnoticed.

> ### ANNE MARIE
> (*eyes screwed shut*)
> Awwwwwoooo, it's stingin'!

> ### MA
> It's naewher near yer eyes.

James slips the packet of cigarettes under the newspaper on the table and goes to leave the room.

> (*to James*)
> Wher dae ye think your gone?

> ### JAMES
> Naewher.

> ### MA
> You've been scratchin' yer heid an' aw.

> ### JAMES
> Naw Ah huvny.

Ma goes over and tips his head forwards.

> ### MA
> (*parting his hair with her fingers*)
> Yuk, yer heid's crawling.

> ### JAMES
> Naw it's no.

Ma walks James backwards. He sits heavily as he bumps the chair.

Da bursts in.

> ### DA
> Wher ur ma fags?
> (*to Ma*)
> Huv ye seen ma fags, Anne?

Ma spots the cigarettes right away.

MA
(gestures to the table)
Well, if you'd look further than the length of yer backside ye
might find them. There they're there.

Da picks up the cigarettes.

DA
Ah looked ther.

*Ma rolls her eyes. Da meekly puts on his suit jacket as he walks over to
the mantelpiece and separates a single note from his pay packet, which
he slyly tucks behind the clock.*

Ther's yer wages, hen.
(going to open the cigarette packet)
Dae ye want me tae leave ye a couple?

*James's head is lying on its side on the kitchen table. His attention is
fixed on the packet in Da's hands.*

MA
Naw, yer awright, Ah've goat some.

*Da pockets the cigarettes and steps aside as Ellen pours water over Anne
Marie's head. Anne Marie howls.*

DA
Right, Ah'm aff. See yous later.

He leaves the kitchen.

(off-screen)
James, take this rubbish doon when yer finished!

JAMES
You take it!

The front door slams. There is a moment of silence in the kitchen.

(into Ma's lap)
Ah goat thim fae hur, minging wee cow.

ANNE MARIE

Naw ye didny. He didny, Ma. He wis scratching his heid
before me!

MA
(*to Ellen*)
Take her out now and get her goony oan her, will ye?

ELLEN
Huv ye heard anything about the new hoose yet, Ma?

MA
(*shakes her head*)

No, hen.

*Ellen looks disappointed. She wraps Anne Marie in a towel and bundles
her out of the room.*

Right, you, keep yer heid doon.

*She pulls the comb roughly through James's hair, her face a mock
grimace.*

Urgghhh.

James cranes his neck up.

JAMES

Let me see thim!

MA

Stay still.

JAMES

Whit dae they look like?

Ma shows him the comb. James examines it.

Ah canny see anything. Wher ur they?

Ma's fingers point towards a clump of tiny white eggs.

(*unimpressed*)

Is that it?

That's the nits ... Look, ther's a wee beast.

She smears a tiny black louse off the comb and shows him it on her finger.

James contentedly rests his head down on the table and closes his eyes.

EXT. KINTRA BACKYARDS. EARLY EVENING

James struggles out of the close carrying two black bin bags. His hair is wet and neatly combed into a parting. He hurls each bag as far as he can over the piles of rubbish.

He leans against the tenement wall and lights up a flattened cigarette from his jacket pocket. He inhales deeply and doubles up coughing.

KENNY
(*off-screen*)
Ye better watch ye don't get lump cancer.

James raises his eyes to the tenement windows. Kenny is looking down at him with his elbows propped on the ledge of an open window.

JAMES

Is that right?

James wanders into the rubbish, fag in hand.

KENNY
Ah'm no allowed to play doon ther. My ma says it's an envir, an enviro –
(*he pauses to think for a moment*)
It's a really mental health hazard ... Guess what?

JAMES
(*uninterested*)

What?

KENNY
Ah bet ye canny guess.

James bends down and picks up a broken brick. He stalks between the bags, his eyes searching for movement.

JAMES

What?

KENNY

Go oan, guess ... Guess!

There is the rustle of movement among the rubbish. James darts over the bags. A glimpse of a tail disappears under another pile. James lobs the brick after it. He steals towards the point of impact. There's nothing there.

Ur you trying tae catch a rat?

JAMES

Naw.

KENNY

They're too fast fur ye. They kin smell ye comin'. Want to see ma present?

JAMES

Whit?

KENNY

It's my birthday.

JAMES
(*monotone*)

Happy birthday.

KENNY

Wait ther, Ah'm comin' doon.
(*he disappears inside the window, then pops his head back out*)
Ur ye waitin'?

James half nods. Kenny disappears again. James climbs down off the pile of bags.

Matt Munroe and his gang approach through the backs. Billy spots James and whistles.

BILLY

Hoi, Jamie, wee man, wher's the bird the day?

JAMES

Whit ye oan aboot?

BILLY

Margaret Anne, ya diddy.

MATT

Ah saw her at Firhill. She was oan her back fur Partick Thistle. Ye better get doon ther soon and sort them out, wee man. The teams ur changing ends at half-time.

The rest of the gang fall about laughing.

Kenny emerges from the close, the top half of his body obscured by a cage he's carrying. Attached to the cage on a string bobs a huge helium balloon embellished with the name 'Kenny'.

Matt Munroe and the gang piss themselves laughing at the sight of Kenny. James backs away, pretending he is nothing to do with him. The boys move from the towpath down to the backs.

TOMMY

Who's yer wee pal, James?

Kenny's legs, the precarious cage and balloon move towards James. Kenny sets the cage down on the ground, revealing himself.

MATT

Look. It's animal boy.

The boys crowd around Kenny. Tommy repeatedly flicks his finger into Kenny's balloon.

TOMMY

Whit huv ye got ther, Kenny?

KENNY

Don't. You'll burst it.

TOMMY

Whit? Ah'm no doing anything.

Tommy continues flicking the balloon while looking innocently at Kenny.

Look. It's a wee rat.

They all peer into the elaborate cage. Inside there are a walking wheel, a water bottle and other toys which dwarf a tiny white mouse which sits in the corner of the cage.

KENNY

It's no a rat!

TOMMY

Whit's its name, Kenny?

KENNY

Snowball.

TOMMY

Aw, that's lovely.

MATT

Let us see it oot.

Kenny contemplates.

KENNY

Do you want to see it, James?

The boys all look towards James, who has backed away from the scene somewhat.

MATT

Aye, you want tae see it, don't you, James?

JAMES

Awright.

BILLY

C'mon, Kenny. James wants tae see it.

TOMMY

Mon, Kenny.

KENNY

Awright, but only James kin hold it.

Kenny reaches into the cage and pulls out the mouse. He walks over to

James and hands the mouse to him. James reluctantly accepts. He strokes its back a few times and quickly hands it back.

                    JAMES
It's nice, Kenny.

                    MATT
Let me see it, Kenny.

The boys crowd round Kenny, who holds the mouse close to his belly.

                    KENNY
No, Ah don't want to.

                    MATT
Aw, c'mon, Kenny. Please?

                    KENNY
It wants tae go back in its cage.

                    MATT
Please, jist fur a wee minute.

                    TOMMY
C'mon, Kenny. Your one of the boys, ay, mate?

                    KENNY
Am I?

                    TOMMY
Aye, an' so is James.

                    KENNY
Are ye, James? Are ye?

James shrugs, feigning coolness in front of the others. Tommy holds his hands out to Kenny with pleading eyes.

OK then, but only for a minute.

He hands the mouse to Tommy, who strokes it. The others gather round him, edging Kenny out of the way. Kenny looks concerned. Billy lifts the mouse by its tail from Tommy's hand and holds it up as it squeaks and wriggles in limbo.

Don't. You'll hurt it.

Billy gently throws the mouse to Matt, who catches it elegantly in his palms.

Gie me it back. You're hurting it.

MATT

Don't worry, Kenny, your mouse is a special mouse, a flying mouse.

Matt throws the mouse a bit further and faster. Billy catches it. Kenny looks like he's going to burst into tears.

KENNY

No. No, don't. Gie me it back, you'll kill it!

He runs towards Billy, but before he reaches him Billy throws the mouse some distance to Matt. The mouse flies effortlessly through the air, claws outstretched, and lands clutching on to Matt's jumper.

MATT

Look, Kenny. Your mouse kin fly.

He throws the mouse to Kenny. Kenny almost falls over trying to catch it.

BILLY

Let it fly to James, Kenny.

TOMMY

Go oan, Kenny!

Kenny looks at the mouse, then to James. He throws the mouse awkwardly and it tumbles through the air towards James.

KENNY

Ma mouse kin fly, James.

James catches the mouse.

Look. Look, ma mouse kin really fly.

TOMMY

Wher is it going tae fly tae, Kenny?

KENNY

Wher will it fly tae, James?

BILLY

Wher is it gonny fly to, James?

JAMES
(*deadpan*)

The moon.

KENNY
(*excited*)

Ma mouse is gonny fly tae the moon.

JAMES

Maybe ye should put it back in its cage, Kenny. It's flown enough the day.

MATT

No yet, Kenny, it's no flown tae the moon yet. Here, James!

James goes to throw the mouse to Matt.

KENNY

No. Let it fly back to me.

James hesitates.

(*excited*)

No, James. Me, me, give it to me.

James gently throws the mouse back to Kenny, who catches it and runs towards the cage.

Kenny holds the mouse in one hand and tugs at the balloon, trying to free it from the cage. He gives up and lifts the cage by the handle.

BILLY

Wher ur ye goin', Kenny?

Kenny rapidly disappears into the close.

MATT

He's mad.

TOMMY
(*mocking Kenny's voice*)
Ma mouse kin fly, ma mouse kin really fly!

The boys collapse into fits of laughter. They all look up towards the tenement on hearing a window opening. Kenny's head pops out.

                              KENNY
Look, James. Look, everybody.

Kenny disappears again. James and the boys stare up at the window, bewildered. Kenny's hands holding the balloon appear over the window ledge. At the end of the balloon's string the white mouse dangles, tied by its tail. Kenny's hands let go of the balloon.

                         (*off-screen*)
Snowball's really going to the moon.

The balloon sinks a little with the weight of the mouse, then steadies and rises slowly upwards into the vivid sunset sky.

    FADE TO BLACK.

FX: the infinite dark void of space, James' dream. Green screen for magic camera special effects.

Music continues.

The 'Kenny' balloon and the tiny mouse drift away from planet Earth towards the moon.

INT. GILLESPIES' LIVING ROOM. EVENING

On the flickering screen of the Gillespies' grainy black-and-white TV set we see an Apollo 11-type image.

The tiny white mouse lands elegantly on the edge of a crater. The mouse scurries off, released on landing from the string of the balloon.

The 'Kenny' balloon floats upwards, framed against the black star-filled sky.

Snowball scrambles into the crater and congregates with the thousands of white mice teeming over the surface of the moon.

INT. LIVING ROOM. NIGHT

Post-transmission TV static flickers and dances on James' sleeping face.

Ma gently lifts James' limp body from the white sofa.

INT. BEDROOM. NIGHT

Ma awkwardly pulls back the covers from the bed, James still sleeping in her arms. She lays him in the bed and covers him.

DAY 7

INT. KITCHEN. DAY

Da is asleep, lying on top of the big bed dressed only in his underpants. We pull back to reveal the debris of breakfast: Rice Krispies, spilt milk, all over the kitchen table.

James is crouched, rummaging in the cupboard under the sink.

INT./EXT. VIEW ON TO KINTRA STREET BACKYARDS FROM GILLESPIES' KITCHEN WINDOW. DAY

From the window we see Margaret Anne in the backyard, smoking a cigarette. She scratches her head with her free hand. She sits down on the low wall of the backs and, resting the smoking cigarette beside her, attacks her scalp with both hands. She scratches intensely, working systematically from the front of her head to the nape of the neck and then out towards her ears.

James removes the bottle of Prioderm lotion, the bar of carbolic soap and the metal comb. He puts the items in his jacket pockets and leaves the kitchen.

From the window we see him wind across the back, through the rubbish bags, to Margaret Anne.

> JAMES
> (*distant*)

When's yer ma back?

> MARGARET ANNE

No tae closin' time.

They leave together along the towpath.

EXT. CANAL. DAY

James and Margaret Anne walk along the canal towpath.

MARGARET ANNE

Marbles oan the floor?

JAMES

Naw, a marble floor. An a big fancy staircase wae seven
bedrooms an a swimming pool.

MARGARET ANNE
(*excited*)

Two swimming pools.

JAMES

Naw, five!

They both laugh.

KENNY
(*off-screen*)

James, James, Ah'm gonny catch a persh!

*Kenny is climbing over the wall ahead of them, clutching a bamboo
cane fishing net and half a sliced white loaf in its bag. He bounds down
the towpath.*

James and Margaret Anne stop in their tracks.

*Kenny crouches down in front of them and starts to roll a slice of bread
into small doughy balls.*

Dae ye think Snowball's oan the moon yet?

JAMES

Ah don't know. Probably.

KENNY
(*standing up*)

I'm gonny throw these in, an' then they'll come an eat them,
an' then I'll catch them.

*He flings the bread into the canal and watches the bobbing white balls
intently.*

One by one they sink without trace.

MARGARET ANNE

Do some more.

Kenny starts to screw up another slice of bread.

James selects a stone from the path and slyly tosses it into the water where Kenny aimed his bread.

> JAMES
> (*awed*)

Whit wis that?

> KENNY

They're bitin'!

Kenny abandons the bread-rolling and cranes towards the water with his net poised to land a whopper.

James motions to Margaret Anne.

> JAMES

Do ya need a hand, Kenny?

> KENNY
> (*eyes fixed forward*)

Naw. Ah'm gonny catch it maself.

Margaret Anne follows James along the towpath.

> MARGARET ANNE

Is he stupid?

James shrugs.

We stay on Kenny, who is preoccupied with his ingenious fishing method.

INT. LIVING ROOM, MARGARET ANNE'S HIGH-RISE FLAT. DAY

Margaret Anne sits cross-legged in the middle of the floor with her head bowed forward.

James kneels behind her, parting her hair with the wetted comb.

> JAMES

Dae ye want to see thim?

James shows her the comb. Margaret Anne screws her eyes up.

MARGARET ANNE

Ah canny see anything. Wher ur they?

He smears a tiny black louse off the comb and shows it to her on his fingertip.

JAMES

Look. Ther's a wee beast. See it?

MARGARET ANNE
(*disappointed*)

Naw.

JAMES

Hang on. I'll find ye a bigger one.
(*he searches through her hair with the comb*)
Look. Ther's a beauty. Kin ye see that one?

He holds his finger close to her eyes.

MARGARET ANNE
(*unsure*)

Aye.

James combs right across her scalp, first one way, then the other. Margaret Anne winces silently as James inexpertly grapples with her countless lice.

JAMES

That's you.

MARGARET ANNE

Huv ye kilt them all?

Margaret Anne's hair looks like she's been dragged through a midden backwards.

JAMES
(*unsure*)
Ah think so. Ye need tae wash it now.

INT. BATHROOM, MARGARET ANNE'S HIGH-RISE FLAT. DAY

Margaret Anne turns the taps on in the bath and starts to undress.

James stands awkwardly with the bar of soap in his hands. He lowers his eyes.

She steps into the bath and sits down with her back to him, waiting.

JAMES

You've got tae wet yer hair first.

Margaret Anne holds her nose and slides under the clear surface of the water, her eyes shut tight. James stares down at her complete nudity.

A moment passes. She rolls over on her stomach. Her body visibly relaxes, her back bobbing up and breaking the surface of the water, her arms drifting limply away from her sides. From buried deep behind the tiled wall the tapping of water clearing in a pipe.

An unnatural amount of time elapses. James's breathing rises. Margaret Anne sits up, exhaling a lungful of air. Her hair is sleeked back from her glowing face.

MARGARET ANNE
(*excited*)

Fifty-seven!

James quickly turns his back to her.

I kin get up tae seventy if Ah count faster!

James gathers Margaret Anne's clothes up from the floor as he regains his composure, deliberately keeping his back to her. He places the clothes on the lid of the toilet pan and turns to dip the soap in the bathwater behind her, keeping his face out of view. Margaret Anne patiently sits with her head bowed forwards. James drops the soap into the bath. He hesitates before he fumbles to retrieve it. Margaret Anne cranes around.

JAMES

Sit still, will ye?

He awkwardly smoothes the bar of carbolic soap over her hair.

He rests the bar of soap on the edge of the bath and silently removes his clothes, gets in the bath behind her, works the soap up to a lather with his hands and rubs it into her hair.

Margaret Anne turns round. Silently understanding, James turns his back to her. She splashes water up his back, James tips his head back.

Margaret Anne rubs the soap into his hair and sculpts it into two little horns. She admires her handiwork and laughs. James feels his hair and laughs.

He turns to face her and sculpts her a mohawk. He works the soap into a foamy tower in his palm and dots it on her nipples.

Peels of childish laughter echo off the tiled walls of the bathroom as they splash and daub each other.

MARGARET ANNE

(*announces*)

Ah need a pee.

She gets out of the bath, matter-of-factly dries her bottom with a towel, and sits on the toilet. She pees noisily with a concentrated expression on her face.

James watches her dumbfounded. Margaret Anne stands up and wipes herself with toilet paper.

Ah'll get ye a towel.

She wraps the towel around her and leaves the room.

INT. LIVING ROOM, MARGARET ANNE'S HIGH-RISE FLAT. DAY

James and Margaret Anne sit on the sofa watching TV with mismatching towels wrapped around their bodies and round their heads like turbans.

Scenes of the strike are on the afternoon local news.

Margaret Anne squints at the TV. They are both halfway through eating identical jam sandwiches.

INT. GILLESPIES' KITCHEN. DAY

Da is sound asleep in the big bed. (Note: like a still photograph.)

Frantic banging is heard off-screen from the front door.

MRS FOWLER
(*off-screen; screaming*)

George ... George!

Da wakes up, disorientated.

DA

What the fu ...

He stumbles out of the kitchen in his underpants, half asleep.

We hear the front door opening.

MRS FOWLER
(*off-screen*)

Help me ... George ... Ma boy ...

DA
(*off-screen*)

Slow doon, hen. Whit's the matter?

MRS FOWLER
(*off-screen*)

He's in ... He's in the canal.

Da runs back into the kitchen. He grabs his trousers from the back of a chair and hops towards the open window as he tries to pull them on. He looks out, the back of his head framed by the clear blue sky and perfect white clouds outside.

(*off-screen; wails from the door*)

Hurry! Hurry!

Da drops his trousers on the floor and runs out of the door. From the window we see a small crowd of children gathered at the bank.

A boy's blue anorak is floating in the middle of the canal, then sinks, releasing a huge bubble of air.

Moments later we see the barefooted Da running through the rubbish-strewn backs in his underpants. He vaults the low wall and dives into the canal, disappearing under the surface.

The water is still. A moment passes.

Da finally emerges at the water's edge with the small boy on his back. He scrambles up the bank, pulling the limp body behind him.

EXT. CANAL TOWPATH. DAY

James is bending over the bank on his knees, poking a stick into the surface of the canal. He lies on his stomach, trying to reach as far out as he can over the water.

A boy cycles past sing-songing.

                         BOY
   Your Da's a hero ...
   Your Da's a hero ...

James looks up at the figure disappearing into the distance.

INT. KITCHEN. DAY

A bottle of whisky is on the kitchen table, a third down.

Da lies uncannily still and corpse-like, his mouth open, on top of the big bed. He is in his underpants and still covered with the dried mud of the canal. James stands transfixed at the foot of the bed.

James notices a trail of blood snaking from Da's toe to collect in a fat drop at the heel of one of his feet. The drop gives with its weight and falls on to the carpet of Rice Krispies on the floor: 'SNAP, CRACKLE, POP'.

James crouches down and gathers a handful of the cereal. He carefully sticks them one by one on to the pattern of congealing blood on Da's feet: 'SNAP, CRACKLE, POP'.

James drops a couple into Da's open mouth. Da stirs. James stands frozen. Da grunts, coughs and then turns on to his side, scratching at his face, still fast asleep.

James stares at the bottle of whisky on the kitchen table.

Offscreen there is a rap at the front door.

James exits the room.

INT. CLOSE/FRONT DOOR. DAY

James opens the door to an official-looking man and woman.

MISS MCDONALD

Is your mother or father in?

JAMES

My da's in, but he's sleeping.

MR MOHAN

We're here from the council. Can we come in?

JAMES

(*excited*)

Is it aboot our new house we're getting?

INT. KITCHEN. DAY

Da is sound asleep, covered in canal dirt and Rice Krispies. Mr Mohan stands peering at the sticky debris of unwashed dishes heaped in the sink. Miss McDonald stands at the head of the table, surveying the aftermath of the kids' breakfast and Da's discarded clothes.

JAMES

Da ... Da ... Wake up ... It's the new hoose people.

Da half stirs.

DA

Get tae ... Leave me in peace ...

JAMES

Da ... Da!

Da jolts upright, disorientated.

DA

(*mumbles*)

Whit the ... Who the fuck are you?

MISS MCDONALD

I'm Miss McDonald and this is Mr Mohan. We've come to inspect the condition of your property and assess your standard of living ... We've obviously caught you at a bad time.

She appraises Da's appearance with an expression of faint amusement. Da suddenly reddens in embarrassment and looks at them apologetically.

DA

Ah've been in the canal ... Mrs Fowler's boy ... I wis in ma bed an' she came to the door in a right state.

MISS MACDONALD
(*patronizing*)

Don't worry, Mr Gillespie, we only want to ask you a few questions and inspect the rest of the premises ...

Da scans the floor for his discarded trousers and edges towards them, vainly attempting to cover himself up with his hands. He awkwardly struggles into his trousers. He wipes Rice Krispies from his feet and nervously rambles on, now standing by the window.

DA

I canny even swim ... I hid tae run through aw that rubbish.
(*he gestures wildly towards the backs*)
Look at it! Look at it! It's a fuckin' disgrace. You know how long this is been goin' oan fur? Eh? Eh? Huv ye seen the state of this place?

MISS MCDONALD

That's not our department, Mr Gillespie. Can we just take a look in the bedrooms?

DA

(*annoyed*)

Well, whose department is it?

Miss McDonald moves towards the door.

I wouldny go in there if I was you. It's a mess, a state.

Da slaps James over the head.

Ya messy wee shite.

JAMES

Ur we getting that big hoose wae two toilets and, and ... a field.

Mr Mohan and Miss McDonald stare blankly at him from across the room.

> MISS MCDONALD
> (*checking against her clipboard*)
> I see it's a three-bedroom property you've applied for, Mr Gillespie.

INT. GILLESPIES' FRONT DOOR. DAY

Da stands in the doorway as the council officials leave. He steals a furtive scratch at his balls.

> MR MOHAN
> (*turning to face Da*)
> If you would just sign here, Mr Gillespie.

Mr Mohan hands him a biro and his clipboard. Da hurriedly extracts his hand from the vicinity of his crotch and signs his name, transferring canal dirt on to the official form. He hands it back to a disdainful Mr Mohan.

> DA
> You'd be better comin' back when the wife's here.

> MISS MCDONALD
> I think we have all the information we need for the moment. Thank you, Mr Gillespie.

> MR MOHAN
> Goodbye.

INT. GILLESPIES' KITCHEN. DAY

Da appears in the kitchen, livid.

> DA
> You ... you canny dae anythin' right, kin ye? Whit did ye let them in fur, eh?

> JAMES
> But Ah thought ...

DA

Go oan, get out of my sight ...

James heads for the door.

JAMES

Ur we getting the new hoose, Da?

DA

It will be your fault if we don't ... Go oan, beat it.

EXT. PAWNSHOP. LATE AFTERNOON

Ellen raps on the shop window above the CLOSED *sign. Mr Mullen comes to the door and unlocks it at the top and bottom.*

Through the window we see Ellen handing him a ticket. He hands Da's suit over the counter to her.

INT. KITCHEN. EARLY EVENING

Da sits on a chair next to the fire in a clean white shirt, socks and underpants. Ma is combing and lacquering his hair. Anne Marie 'polishes' his shoes in the corner with large dollops of blackening.

Da tips his head back to scratch at his throat.

MA

Wid ye hoad still a minute. Whit's the matter wae you?

DA

Ah'm aw itchy. Huv ye finished yet?

MA

Jist a minute.

Ma shoots a last dense spray of lacquer over Da's hair as Da impatiently gets out of the chair.

Awright, that's you.

Da splashes aftershave liberally on his face and neck.

DA

Ooooooaaaaargh!

76

Margaret Mullen says the council inspectors turned up tae
see her hoose today. They didny come round here, did they?

*Da walks over to his shaving mirror and fiddles at his tie with his back
to her.*

DA

Who?

*He smoothes down his hair with his hands and starts scratching
violently at his face.*

MA

Thank God for that.

Ellen enters the kitchen carrying Da's suit from the pawnshop.

ELLEN

He didny take any money for it.

She goes to hand Da fifty pence.

DA

You keep it, hen.

ELLEN
(eyes widen)

Really? Thanks, Da ... He told me to tell ye you're a hero.

DA
(self-satisfied)

Did he?

*There is a knock on the door. Ellen goes to answer. Da pulls on his suit
trousers. Ma helps him into the jacket. Mrs Fowler bursts into the
kitchen and rushes over to Da.*

MRS FOWLER

George, George.

DA

Come on in, hen ...

MRS FOWLER

My hero.

(she pecks him on the cheek)

This is fur you.

She offers Da a ten-pound note.

DA

Don't be daft.

MRS FOWLER

Just take it.

She tries to put the tenner in his jacket pocket. Da pushes her hand away.

DA

Och, away you go.

Mrs Fowler places the tenner on the table.

MRS FOWLER

I'll leave it here, then ... Ah canny thank you enough, George.

MA

How's the boy?

MRS FOWLER

Fine. No a scratch on him. Thank you, George ... thank you.

DA

Och, away ye go ... You're embarrassing me.

Mrs Fowler tiptoes backwards to the door and draws it to behind her.

Och, that wuman, she's making such a big fuss.

MA
(smiles knowingly)
Ah think yer enjoyin' it really. Look at the face on you.

DA
(feigned annoyance)
Ah jist want tae go fur a quiet pint.

ANNE MARIE

Here's yer shoes, Daddy.

Da bends down to Anne Marie's height and takes the shoes and the chamois from her.

Kin Ah get fifty pence tae?

Da wipes the clods of polish off the toes of the shoes. He slyly opens Ma's purse from the table and hands Anne Marie a fifty-pence coin.

(*eager*)

Yesss.

She waves her money in the air and makes a smug face at Ellen.

Ellen draws her a dirty look.

DA

Where's that James?

Ma goes over to the open window.

MA
(*at the top of her voice*)
James ... James ... James Gillespie.

There is no answer.

DA

Wher does that boy get tae?

MA

Ah don't know, but Ah'm gonny kill him when he gets in; his tea's freezin'.

DA
(*scratching violently again*)
Ah'm aff then. See ye later.

Anne Marie jumps up into Da's arms for a kiss. He swings her down and heads for the door.

INT./EXT. BACKYARDS/GILLESPIES' CLOSE. EARLY EVENING

James is cutting through the close to the backs, scraping an old blackened poker along the wall, as Da reaches the bottom of the stairwell.

DA
(shouts)

Hi, you! Wher do you think yer gone?

James whips around, startled.

Get up the stairs, yer Ma's lookin' fur you.

James slopes towards the bottom stair, avoiding eye contact with Da.

So what do you think of yer da, eh?

James climbs a step without reply.

Da disappears into the street.

JAMES

An arse.

He turns around and runs back down the stairs.

EXT. DUKE STREET CANAL. EARLY EVENING

James, leaning over the water, is trying to hook Margaret Anne's glasses, which are caught in the rusted skeleton of an old mattress. He inadvertently pushes them deeper into the cavernous springs and out of his reach.

DAY 8

INT. TOWN HALL. DAY

A crowded hall. The audience sit on neat rows of wooden benches. From the stage the Lord Provost of Glasgow is delivering a general address on the good deeds and bravery of the children of the city.

James sits stiff and uncomfortable, his hair neatly combed and his face clean and shiny. He fiddles with his too-tight collar, trying to unbutton it.

In the row beside him sit Anne Marie, Ellen and Ma, dressed up in their best clothes. Da sits next to the aisle, looking especially odd, his face dotted with small red scabs caught from the canal.

KENNY

(*Off-screen; whispered*)

James ... James!

Mrs Fowler and Kenny, his face also dotted with bright red scabs, sit in the row across the aisle.

Kenny is craning across to gain James's attention.

James, James, do ye think Snowball's oan the moon yet?

James ignores him.

MRS FOWLER

(*whispered*)

Shut up. If I hear one more thing aboot that moose ...

She clouts Kenny on the back of the head, then turns round haughtily and draws James an accusing look. James looks away guiltily. He eavesdrops on Ellen and Ma whispering.

ELLEN

Even Mrs Mullen's moving.

MA

We'll hear soon.

ELLEN

But you always say tha ...

MA

Sshhhh.

Ellen grimaces. Anne Marie turns to a woman sitting behind them.

ANNE MARIE

My da's a hero.

The woman smiles politely and turns back to speak to her friend.

LORD PROVOST

Now would those here to receive commendations come forward.

Sir William Walton's 'Dam Busters Theme' blasts out of the PA.

Da leaps to his feet, intent on beating the horde of 'brave' children gathering in the aisle leading to the stage.

MA

C'mere. Ah'll fix yer tie.

Da is barely stood up straight before Ma is pulling the knot back up to his throat.

Mrs Fowler grabs Da's dangling hand from behind.

MRS FOWLER

Ah canny thank ye enough, George. When Ah think aboot whit might have happened if you hadny been ther ...

DA

(*embarrassed*)

Nae bother, Gina.

He tries to pull away, his eye on the dozens of kids, some encumbered by slings and crutches, being stewarded on to the stage.

Mrs Fowler plants a big kiss on Da's cheek, leaving a greasy red lipstick imprint.

MRS FOWLER

Kenny, Kenny, whit huv ye goat tae say tae Mr Gillespie?

KENNY

Ah sent Snowball to the moon, Mr Gillespie, so Ah did. Didn't Ah, James?

Mrs Fowler clouts Kenny over the head.

MRS FOWLER

What did Ah tell ye! ... That's the last time I get you anythin' ... Just you wait.

KENNY

(*rehearsed, his eyes welling up*)

Thanks a lot, Mr Gillespie. Thanks a lot for savin' ma wife ... Ah mean life.

Da finally wrenches himself free and saunters down the aisle.

Anne Marie turns back to the woman behind her and catches her sleeve.

ANNE MARIE

Missus ... Missus, that's him ther, that's my da.

Anne Marie frantically points to the front of the hall. Kenny waves at Da in floods of tears.

KENNY
(*sobbing*)

Thanks, Mr Gillespie, thanks a lot for savin' me.

Mrs Fowler hushes him.

LORD PROVOST
(*reading from Da's certificate*)

To George Gillespie for bravery.

Da scratches his face nervously as the Lord Provost pins a shining gold medal hanging from a green and gold ribbon to the lapel of his jacket.

Everybody cheers.

Da floats down the aisle between the rows of benches, looking a bit pale. He leans over to Ma.

DA

Geese ma coat over, hen, Ah'm away fur a pint.

James eyes Da suspiciously.

MA

Don't be too long, George, I've goat somethin' nice in fur yer tea.

DA
(*to James*)

Whit ur you lookin' at?

JAMES

Yer scabs.

Da gives James an 'I'll deal with you later' point of his finger and walks off.

EXT./INT. PUB. DAY

Da is stopped as he goes to push the pub door open by a trampy adolescent holding a flabby plastic bag.

Hi, mister, ur you a war hero?

The boy points to Da's medal. Da smiles and goes to push the door.

Hang oan a minute, mister. Ah've goat somethin' here you
might be interested in.

*He fishes in the plastic bag and produces a grubby pair of used football
boots with* PARTICK THISTLE F.C. *emblazoned on their sides. Da
inspects the boots.*

DA

They'd be too wee fur me, son ... Anyway, Ah support the
green and whites maself.

FRANKIE

Put it there, comrade.

The boy holds out his hand. Da shakes it firmly.

Whit aboot yer boy? Whid they no fit him?

DA

They look a bit big fur him.

FRANKIE

Aw, c'mon, mister, he'll grow intae them. He'll be playing
like Jimmy Johnson before ye know it. Yiv goat tae start them
aff young, take it fae me.

Da contemplates the offer.

Only ten bob. They're a steal.

Da goes to push the pub door again.

DA

Och, away ye go, son.

FRANKIE

Awright, awright, two bob, that's ma final offer.

*Da gives in. He hands the boy a coin and accepts the plastic bag. The
boy goes to follow Da into the pub.*

They'll no serve you in here, son.

Da pushes the pub door.

FRANKIE

Want tae bet?

Frankie follows Da in.

A cheer goes up as Da enters the pub.

ANDY
(off-screen)

Get that man a pint.

INT. LIVING ROOM. DAY

Ma fixes the needle on the record. Eddie Cochrane's 'C'mon, Everybody' crackles from the record player. Loud and jumpy.

James, Ellen and Anne Marie sit on the white leatherette sofa, a bowl of crisps between them.

ANNE MARIE
(whine)
Ah wanted Tom Jones. Turn it off, turn it off...

MA
Och, you lot widny know a good tune if it came up an bit ye.

ANNE MARIE
(at the top of her voice)
Tom Jones, Tom Jones, Tom Jones.

Ellen holds her fingers in her ears.

ELLEN

Aw, shut up, will ye?

JAMES
Tom Jones is shite, Anne Marie.

ANNE MARIE
Naw he's no. He's brilliant. You're shite, you're a big shite.

85

Right, you two, that's enough. Ah don't want tae hear that
kind of language in ma hoose, do ye hear me, young lady?

ANNE MARIE
(*sulky*)

He said it first.

JAMES

Da swears aw the time.

MA

Right, you lot, who's up for a dance?
                    (*at the top of her voice*)
'C'mon, everybody'.

They all stare up at Ma blankly from the sofa.

I'll dance maself.
(*she takes the handle of the living-room door and starts jiving*)
Me an yer da were the best jivers at the Lindella.

They all snigger on the sofa.

ELLEN
(*covering her eyes*)

No way.

JAMES

She's mad.

MA

Is that right. Ah bet ye you couldny dae it.
                    (*she sashays over to the sofa*)
Ur ye dancin'?

JAMES

No.

MA

Yer meant tae say, 'Ur ye asking'?' So, ur ye dancin'?

JAMES

No way.

Ma tries to pull the very reluctant James off the sofa.

Ma ... Leave me alain ...Ma, stoap it ... don't ...

                    MA
C'mon, you, up ye get.

She gets him up and starts twirling him round and round.

                ANNE MARIE
                (sing-song)
James canny jive, James canny jive.

Ma swings James through her legs. James collapses on the floor in fits of laughter.

EXT. PUB. DAY

Da is prising the inebriated Rita's arms from around his neck.

                    DA
Ah've goat tae git hame, hen.

                   RITA
                (bawling)
Don't leave me, George. Yer not gonny leave me, ur ye?

                    DA
I'm jist gone hame.

                   RITA
                (tearful)
Naw, stay, mon, we'll huv another drink, ye canny leave me.

                    DA
                (exasperated)
Here, take this.

He takes a crumpled pound note from his jacket pocket and presses it into her hand. She stumbles back through the pub door, looking crestfallen.

EXT. STREET. EARLY EVENING

Da, whisky-intoxicated, staggers up the street. He hums in time to the theme from Dr Zhivago, *the familiar jingle of the local ice-cream van. A small girl holding a scruffy kitten approaches him. He smiles.*

GIRL

Mister, gonny hold ma cat, while I get a cone fae the van?

DA

Sure, hen.

Da props himself up against the wall of a tenement to wait for her.

Five teenage boys pass by and laugh at the image of the drunken man with the kitten's head poking out from the inside of his jacket.

(*slurred*)

Aw, fuck off, the lot ay ye.

The boys double back.

Who the fuck ur you lookin' at, ya cheeky wee bastard?

The boys engulf him, pinning him against the wall. A filed metal comb is produced from a corduroy back pocket. It slashes down Da's chin.

The boys flee, laughing.

Big globules of blood run off Da's chin. He stoops to vomit. The bloodied kitten falls from his jacket and bolts in fright.

Little rivers of melting ice-cream and raspberry sauce run between the small girl's fingers. She licks her hand clean as she watches Da stagger up the street holding his chin together with his hand.

INT. KITCHEN. NIGHT

A Mr Kipling iced cake stands in the centre of the kitchen table. James is picking at the icing.

Off-screen we can hear the crashing and thumping of Ma, Ellen and Anne Marie dancing to Little Millie's 'My Boy Lollipop' in the living room.

Da crashes through the front door and in to the kitchen, holding his bleeding face with his hand. He is drunk, silent and filled with fury.

Da throws the plastic bag towards James. The grubby football boots spill out.

Try them oan.

James stares at the boots.

Try them oan.

JAMES

Ah don't want tae.

DA

I bought them fur you, ye ungrateful wee swine.

James reluctantly puts on the boots. His feet slip into them easily without untying the laces. They are ridiculously big for him.

James kicks the boots off towards Da. They bounce hard off Da's chest.

JAMES

Ah don't like fitba.

Da's eyes stare madly.

Ma enters the kitchen. She sees the dripping blood and tries to get Da to show her the wound.

MA

Aw, no again ... Let me see.

She pulls his hand away and gasps. Da slaps her hard across the face. Ma's cheek burns red. They stand like statues for a moment, both shocked.

Off-screen we hear the front door slam shut as James leaves the flat.

EXT. BACKYARDS. EARLY EVENING

Brazen rats intermittently dart across the small clearing at the base of a mountain of rubbish bags. At its summit, James clutches the blackened poker with both hands.

He charges towards the movement and lunges with the poker. A metallic noise rings out around the backs as it strikes the concrete ground. James kicks the surrounding bags away from its tip. A huge rat is lanced right through its belly.

James catches his breath; he is as white as a sheet. The dead rat lies still, its limbs frozen.

INT. LIFT, MARGARET ANNE'S HIGH-RISE. NIGHT

The numbers over the door light up in sequence. They stop at the ninth floor. The doors rattle open. James hesitates, staring into the landing. The doors shut. He presses the '9' button again. The door opens, he walks out.

INT. LANDING OF THE NINTH FLOOR. NIGHT

James walks over to Margaret Anne's front door. Behind him another door opens and an old woman walks out to the lift. James rings the bell. The old woman is staring at him from across the landing. James chaps Margaret Anne's letter box. A moment passes.

Margaret Anne opens the door, looking like she's just woken up.

INT. MARGARET ANNE'S BEDROOM. NIGHT

Margaret Anne and James sit on her single bed in the sparse bedroom, leaning their backs against the wall. Margaret Anne smokes a cigarette. She offers a puff of it to James. James inhales the cigarette and coughs.

Off-screen, the sound of the front door opening.

JAMES

Is that yer ma?

Off-screen, drunken footsteps stumble haltingly along the hallway.

MARGARET ANNE

Don't worry. She'll no come in. Put the light aff.

James turns off the light. Margaret Anne pulls the covers over her and lies down.

Ah'm freezin'.

James sits on the edge of the bed.

Ur ye no gettin' in?

James gets in beside her. She cuddles him.

Dae ye love me?

JAMES

Aye.

They both close their eyes.

INT. GILLESPIES' LIVING ROOM. NIGHT

*'Something Stupid', by Frank and Nancy Sinatra, plays in the
background. Ma and Da dance close, holding each other tight. They
slowly spin. Da's scar is butterfly-stitched. He mumbles apologies into
Ma's ear and strokes her hair. Ma looks into the distance, then closes
her eyes.*

DAY 9

EXT. KINTRA STREET. EARLY MORNING

The sun spreads over the empty street. The sound of a distant rumble.

*At the bottom of the street a khaki cloth-covered army truck comes into
view, followed by two others. They trundle slowly and noisily up the
street.*

*The trucks come to a standstill. Soldiers carrying long metal spikes pile
out of the back of the trucks and gather on the pavement. The legs of
their trousers are tied tight against their ankles with string. They pull
green-cloth masks over their mouths and noses.*

The sergeant directs groups of five into separate closes.

INT. KITCHEN, MARGARET ANNE'S FLAT. EARLY MORNING

James stands watching at the window.

POV: VIEW FROM MARGARET ANNE'S HIGH RISE TO KINTRA
BACKYARDS.

*Ant-size soldiers pour from the closes into the tenement backs along the
canal.*

EXT. KINTRA BACKYARDS. DAY

Soldiers lift the bags methodically, exposing rats that dart and flee, disorientated, deeper into the pile.

Faces gather to watch from the tenement windows. The sound of many windows opening.

ARTIE
(*shouts to soldiers*)

Scabs ... fuckin' scabs, the lot a ye.

JESSE

Aw, shut yer face, you.

ARTIE

Mind yer ain business, ya torn-faced auld cow.

JESSE
(*laughs*)

Sat oan your fat arses fur the last three months, letting the place turn into a pigsty ... Yer even scared tae let the weans play in the backs.

ARTIE
(*sanctimonious*)

Hoi, you –

One of the soldiers looks up.

Aye, you, son. Yer takin' away a man's livelihood. Ah hope ye know that.

JESSE

Och, let the boys get oan wae their job.

There are cheers of affirmation from other windows.

Someone wolf-whistles. A soldier looks up.

WOMAN'S VOICE
(*off-screen*)

Awright, handsome.

Laughter resounds.

A soldier spikes a rat. He holds it up to inspect it. Boys gather round him; among them is Kenny.

BOYS

Let us see it, mister ... Look at it ... It's the size ay a cat ...

The boys disperse, returning with sticks and 'domestic' weapons.

BOY

(*to the soldiers*)

Kin we help you kill 'em?

SOLDIER

Naw, son, we can manage.

The boys heed no warning. They clamber round the soldiers, beating the bags with sticks and chasing fleeing rats. Anne Marie walks out of the close.

ANNE MARIE

Gonny see if ye kin find ma doll in ther, mister?

BOYS

Yahoo ... Get it ... Look, ther's wan ...

INT. HALLWAY, MARGARET ANNE'S FLAT. DAY

James walks down the hallway, passing an open door. He stops, catching sight of Rita, who is sprawled asleep fully clothed on top of the double bed. Her mouth is agape, her lips and eyes blurred with last night's make-up.

He stands in the doorway, staring at her contorted body, then walks down the hall.

One of Rita's scuffed high heels lies beside her open handbag on the floor by the front door. The contents are strewn messily over the floor: bits of make-up, scrunched-up tissues, a few coins and coppers.

James picks up a sticky ten-pence piece from the carpet.

He quietly closes the door behind him as he leaves the flat.

EXT. KINTRA STREET. DAY

Children are gathered round the trucks and are trying to climb inside.

SOLDIER
C'mon, you lot, get doon fae ther.

A small girl puts her arms round a soldier's leg.

GIRL
Gonny let me see ... Please.

The soldier gives in and lifts her up into the back of the army truck. The children crowd round them.

CHILDREN
Me next, mister! ... Ah want up ... It's ma turn ...

Ellen appears from the entrance of the close and walks up to one of the soldiers. She bats her eyelids, feigning shyness.

ELLEN
(in her best voice)
Hello ... My mother made you some tea. She's bringing it down to the back. She told me to tell you.

SOLDIER
Thanks, hen.

Ellen laughs nervously.

ELLEN
Everybody thinks you're all brilliant.

The soldier looks around nervously.

SOLDIER
Thanks, hen, we're jist doin' our job.

ELLEN
Well, em, see you later.

Ellen, doe-eyed, walks off backwards, almost tripping up.

EXT. BACKYARDS. DAY

James approaches the backs. He is met with a scene of surreal disorder.

Slow motion: among a group of a dozen boys Kenny charges about on the periphery of an attack on the rats, swinging a dead rat by the tail.

One boy pounds eagerly and viciously down on a half-spilled bag.

>   BOY
>   (*breathless and gleeful*)
> Ah goat it. It's deed!

The rest of the boys gather round to study the dead rat.

>   KENNY
> Ah'm gonny kill wan tae!

He leaps on top of a bag, his eyes searching for a potential victim.

He spots James and waves the rat in the air above his head.

>   (*mouthed; the soundtrack fades*)
> James! James! Look.

He turns away, involved again in the game of catching another rat.

A rat runs to and fro, unable to escape, cornered.

James walks through the back towards the close, invisible to the preoccupied residents.

INT. KITCHEN. DAY

Butterfly stitches map an angry red scar on Da's chin. He tidies his shirt into his trousers and fixes his hair, posing for Ma, who holds a Polaroid camera to her eye.

>   MA
> You better go an look for him.

>   DA
> Och, he'll be fine.

>   MA
> Ah'm worried sick.

95

DA

Och, he'll be awright. He kin look efter himself. Ah wis always running aff when Ah wis a boy ... Ur ye gonny take ma picture ur whit?

MA

This is stupid.

DA

You'll no be saying that when Ah get ma damages.

MA

You'll no get ah penny. That's just a scratch.

DA

Criminal injuries. Andy goat a wad when that boy kicked his heid in doon the pub.

MA

You should have tried tae get them for the big one ... Ur you no gonny smile or something?

DA

Don't be daft. This is serious.

Da holds his hard-man pose, hands on his hips, chin raised up, a mean look on his face. Ma takes a picture, but the flash doesn't go off.

Aw, fur fuck's sake, kin ye no even work a bloody instamatic camera?

Ma studies the camera.

MA

It's no ma fault, thir must be something up wae it.

DA

Och, geese it here, woman.

He grabs the camera from Ma.

MA

Bloody dae them yerself then.

Da studies the camera.

DA

Ye didny even switch the flash button oan, ya idiot.

Ma walks over to the window. Da studies the underexposed Polaroid.

Och, that's nae good. You'll need tae dae another one.

MA

Wher is he?

DA
(off-screen)

Ah don't know, but when Ah get ah hoad of him Ah'll kill the wee bastard.

Off-screen the front door slams.

MA

James?

Cutaway: in real time we see a discarded Polaroid of Da developing.

EXT. FROM KINTRA BACKYARDS. DAY

We see Ma at the window of the Gillespies' kitchen.

MA
(mouthed; silent)

James!

INT./EXT. GILLESPIES' LIVING-ROOM WINDOW ON TO KINTRA STREET. DAY

We see Ma's POV of James running and getting on to a bus.

INT. THE TOP DECK OF THE BUS. LATE AFTERNOON

James is upstairs on the front seat of the moving bus. The landscape outside the window transforms from urban streets to hedgerows and open countryside. Spits of rain begin to patter on the window.

EXT. ROW OF HOUSES, EASTERHOUSE. LATE AFTERNOON

Heavy rain. James is soaking wet. He walks down a concrete path between the two rows of the smart new houses. The row of empty houses is more complete than before; doors have been put on and there is glass in the window frames. The concrete path ends abruptly at the small empty building site.

James walks to the door of the last house on the row (the same house he had previously explored). He turns the handle but the door is locked.

EXT. BACK OF HOUSE, SUMMERSTON FIELD. LATE AFTERNOON

He walks round to the back of the house. The back door is also locked. He hauls himself on to the window ledge. The window has been glassed up. He peers through into the empty kitchen, which is much as it had been before.

INT./EXT. NEW SCHEME HOUSE. LATE AFTERNOON

From the vista of the kitchen window, we see James walking in the distance as he cuts diagonally through the field. The sound of heavy rain as it raps hard on the window-pane. The sky is gun-metal grey, the wheat in the field bows and sways in great waves in the wind.

EXT. RIVER BANK. LATE AFTERNOON

The rain thuds dimples into the torrid river. James pees into the water. Heavy drops collect on his eyebrows and lashes, and streak down his cheeks. He sits on the bank, soaked, watching the angry flow of the current.

EXT. KINTRA STREET. EARLY EVENING

The deserted street is hardly recognizable, cleared of black bags and litter. James is an isolated figure walking up the street.

EXT. KINTRA BACKYARDS. EARLY EVENING

Much of the rubbish has been cleared. The rest has been moved to one side, leaving half of the concrete floor of the backyard visible again. Kenny follows James. Running to catch up, he holds a dead rat like a trophy. James ignores him and makes for the old coal bunker, which has been freshly bricked up. He hears squeaking from the thin gap between the top of the new bricks and the slab roof. He hoists himself up and, lying face down on the roof, tips his head over the edge to peer through.

98

Inside the deep bunker, dozens of rats clamber over one another in the darkness, covered in powdered blue poison.

KENNY

(*off-screen*)

James!

James looks down.

Kenny is standing below him, dangling the dead rat by its tail. He holds it up to James for inspection.

Look. Ah kilt it.

JAMES

Ah thought you were a member of the RSPCA.

KENNY

(*bewildered*)

Ma ma says their verm . . . verm . . . um . . . pests.

James says nothing. Kenny tries to think of something to say.

Yer ma's lookin' fur you.

James ignores him. Kenny looks up at the sky beyond James and points to the sun.

Lookit the moon.

James rolls over and stands up. Kenny waves.

Hello, Snowball.

JAMES

Snowball's deed, Kenny.

Kenny stares blankly past him at the moon.

BILLY

(*off-screen*)

Whit's aw this Ah've been hearing aboot you?

From his vantage point, James looks down into the adjacent backyard. Billy and Tommy are loitering around the outside toilet. James steps from the top of the bunker on to the dividing wall of the backs.

99

JAMES

Whit ye oan aboot?

TOMMY

Up at yer bird's hoose aw night!

BILLY

Whooooaaahhhh. Ladies' man, eh?

TOMMY
(*winks*)
Put a smile oan her face, did ye, eh?

BILLY

She sayed yur gettin' married.

JAMES

Yer talkin' shite.

BILLY

That's whit she told us.

Tommy starts banging at the toilet door.

JAMES

Well, she's a stupid cow.

The door opens a fraction.

TOMMY

Yer fiancée wants a word.

Margaret Anne is shoved out of the toilet. She tugs her skirt down. Matt Munroe follows her.

MARGARET ANNE

Whit?

MATT MUNROE
Tell us whit James sayed tae ye last night.

MARGARET ANNE
(*quietly*)

He loves me.

The boys can barely contain themselves.

JAMES

That's shite. Yer nothin' but a pure cow.

KENNY
(*off-screen*)

You're a pure cow, pure cow, purecow, purecow, poorcow, poorcow . . .

THE BOYS
(*in unison*)

Did yer hear whit he called ye, Margaret Anne?

KENNY
(*off-screen*)

Poorcow, purrkow, purkow . . .

THE BOYS

Tell him to fuck off.

MATT MUNROE

Go oan.

BILLY

Say it. Go oan.

MARGARET ANNE

Fuck off.

JAMES

Shut up, Kenny.

KENNY
(*off-screen*)

Fuckodd, Fuckodd fuckodd, foookgod . . .

The boys all fall about laughing. Kenny mimics them off-screen, roaring louder than anyone.

BILLY

Mon, hen, it's ma turn.

Margaret Anne compliantly follows Billy into the toilet.

EXT. CANAL TOWPATH. DUSK

James sprints along the edge of the canal, his face straining against the rush of air. Faster and faster along the bank.

EXT. CANAL TOWPATH. NIGHT

James walks aimlessly. His eyelids are heavy and he is exhausted. He sits down on the road. He lies on his side.

Later: James wakes with a start. A big stray dog is sniffing at him, slobbering over his face. Startled, he is immediately on his feet. The dog backs away and scarpers.

INT. HALLWAY, KINTRA CLOSE. NIGHT

James enters the darkened hallway, gently closes the front door behind him and tiptoes towards the living room.

INT. LIVING ROOM. NIGHT

James lies on the sofa, exhausted but awake.

Anne Marie walks into the room in her nightgown. She is barely awake, rubbing her eyes, mumbling and whining imperceptible words. She makes a beeline for the sofa and flops down next to James. With the same reflex she deposits her arm on to him and is instantly asleep.

Initially James pulls away from her and lies as stiff as a board, uncomfortable with the uninvited intimacy. He delicately tries to remove her arm; she moans a little and her eyelashes flutter. He hasn't the heart to wake her and resigns himself to her clinging little arm. He looks away from her. Slowly he allows himself to study her face. Flawless as only a child's can be, grubby and tear-stained, her mouth is a little open and she snores lightly in a childish way.

A tear wells in James's eye. Without intimation his body heaves into spasms of grief. He cries, unintimidated and unabashed with an utter lack of self-consciousness. Anne Marie lies by his side, blissfully unaware.

Exhausted, James's eyelids fall. He unconsciously puts his arm around Anne Marie. The two children lie together, asleep.

DAY 10

INT. LIVING ROOM. DAWN

Taking care not to disturb her, James disentangles himself from Anne Marie and silently leaves the room.

EXT. DUKE STREET CANAL. DAWN

James is on his knees, bending over the bank, poking a long stick into the canal. He lies on his stomach, trying to reach as far out as he can over the water.

Under water: Margaret Anne's lost glasses caught in the springs of the old mattress. The distorted silhouette of James above the surface poking the stick towards them. It is nowhere near long enough to reach them. As he prods at the springs, the glasses loosen and fall, receding out of sight in the murk.

James lowers himself into the water feet first from the bank. The water is immediately up to his waist. He calmly steps forward, feeling for a footing. He is shoulder deep when, without warning, the bottom suddenly disappears beneath his feet. His body totally submerges. He quickly reappears. Terrified, he struggles to keep his head above the black water. He dips under again, choking a little as he surfaces. The struggle continues, his head dipping under and surfacing quickly. He flails his arms for dear life in an attempt to move towards the safety of the shallows.

EXT. CANAL TOWPATH. DAY

Da's face stares blankly straight ahead, his features red and distorted. Perspiration beads on his brow and runs on to his cheeks and into his eyes. He stumbles and grimaces. His shoulders strain as he readjusts his grip on the end of the white leatherette sofa.

The sun and clouds are reflected on the still surface of the canal. Da and Boaby carry the sofa between them along the towpath.

They lead a procession of men carrying items of furniture along the canal bank.

Further behind, Ma and Ellen carry smaller items; their faces stare blankly ahead.

Anne Marie dawdles, carrying a mirror in front of her like a tray.

EXT. WHEAT FIELD. DAY

The clouds and blue sky reflect in the surface of Anne Marie's mirror. The surreal procession of furniture bearers continues through the golden wheat field by the river, towards the new houses.

INT./EXT. KITCHEN IN NEW HOUSE LOOKING ON TO FIELD. DAY

The procession of furniture bearers moves closer.

EXT. SUMMERSTON FIELD. DAY

A way behind walks James, a chair carried high on his shoulders.